mom,
you make a
difference!

mom,
you make a
difference!

encouraging reminders
from real moms

MOPS International

Edited by Elisa Morgan

Revell
Grand Rapids, Michigan

© 2005 by MOPS International

Published by Fleming H. Revell
a division of Baker Publishing Group
P.O. Box 6287, Grand Rapids, MI 49516-6287

Printed in the United States of America

Library of Congress Cataloging-in-Publication Data
Mom, you make a difference! : encouraging reminders from real moms / edited by Elisa Morgan.
       p.   cm.
   ISBN 0-8007-5998-2 (hardcover)
   1. Mothers—Religious life. I. Morgan, Elisa, 1955– II. Title.
BV4529.18.M65 2005
306.874′3—dc22   2004022812

Published in association with the literary agency of Alive Communications, Inc., 7680 Goddard Street, Suite 200, Colorado Springs, CO 80920.

contents

· · · · · · · · · · · · · · · · · ·

Contents

. . . .

introduction

MOMS NEED CONTINUOUS encouragement, inspiration, and insight as they raise their children in our ever-changing world. This book is a compilation of thought-provoking email messages written by more than thirty-five seasoned mothers reflecting on topics such as: asking for help, time away, making special memories, and treasuring those extraordinary moments with kids.

In spring 2001, MOPS International (Mothers of Preschoolers) created weekly Mom-E-Mails to communicate with moms who joined the MOPS♥to♥Mom Connection. Every Monday, tens of thousands of moms receive an encouraging email that brings a fresh perspective on raising kids. These inspiring pieces challenge mothers to make choices with their kids that will make a difference for tomorrow.

Take time to sit back and read a chapter or two. When you're finished, pass it on to a friend. These life-changing messages may make you laugh or cry, but most of all, they will encourage you to remember that mothering always matters.

part one

no one
like mom

the "specialist" mom

. . . .

YOU'RE THE 'SPECIALIST' MOM in the world!"

What wonderful words to see and hear! My daughter, who has inherited a "craft" gene that somehow bypassed me, wrote those words on an elaborate card she proudly made all by herself. As I was reorganizing my many piles the other day, I rediscovered those beautiful words and her creative handiwork. Reading them made me stop and think not just of her, but how blessed I really am to be a mom.

I see the smiles on my kids' faces as we spontaneously pile into the car for ice cream. Their joy as they come to the table to see their "favorite food" for dinner, their excitement to see me after I have been gone on a trip or even just a long day. Small things, but these are powerful reminders that my presence in their lives is making a difference for always.

I sometimes have days that make me feel as if I'm standing next to a merry-go-round, trying to grab hold of a horse to get on. However, the merry-go-round keeps spinning faster and faster, and no matter what I do, it keeps getting away. When the laundry is piled high, there are one too many carpools to drive, and I'm at yet another meeting where I need to be more than physically present—it's on those days that I need the reminder, "You're the 'specialist' mom in the world!" That is what stops the merry-go-round just long enough for me get on and appreciate the rich colors and variety that my life as mom has to offer.

Take a minute today to "enjoy the ride" with your child.

~ Michele Hall

the birthday present
• • • • • • • • • • • • • • • •

MY SON'S BIRTHDAY was fast approaching . . . and I had to get going on his present.

I had a special plan that year. For two years, Josh had been asking for his very own kitten. So far I had resisted, but after so much time I realized that this "ask" was something Josh really wanted. No other gift would mean more to him.

So, off I went with my daughter to a nearby animal shelter, all set to buy the perfect kitten . . . only to find that all of the kittens had been spoken for. A bit unsure what to do next, we roamed into the "sick ward" of the shelter and there she was: a pretty and personable eleven-month-old kitty with a cold, watching every move we made. Lindsey and I both knew immediately—this particular kitty needed us. Other "well" kittens would be snatched up, but this slightly older, slightly sick, slightly worn-out kitten needed a good home.

We managed to sneak her home that night and hide her from Josh until the morning of his birthday. What a surprise! Josh exclaimed over and over in disbelief, "This is MY kitty?" And it was love at first sight on both sides. Within minutes, that kitty was following Josh all over the house, sitting on his lap, purring, licking him, and acting like she had found her long lost buddy. What a thrill that these two had found each other!

As I reflect now, Josh's birthday present reminds me of the first few moments between mother and child. When we see our children for the first time, it is love at first sight. And it doesn't matter if we moms are slightly older, slightly sick, slightly worn-out. Our children love us right back.

God chose YOU to be your child's mother. You are God's special gift for your child—maybe a bit tired or less-than-perfect at times, but still a perfect fit—just like Josh and his kitty.

~ Cyndi Bixler

instinct and instruction

WE LIVE ON A CATTLE RANCH in the Nebraska Sandhills, and for us, February is the beginning of calving season. I love this time of year, when I can ride out to check on the mama cows and their calves snuggled in the hay. As a mom, I feel sorry for the cows as they give birth without a coach to help them breathe or empathize with their pain. Yet once a baby calf is born, a mama cow instinctively knows what to do—she removes the afterbirth from around the calf's nose and mouth so it can breathe, she nudges her baby to get up and walk, and she knows right away how to feed her calf. Mama cows are protective of their young; they let anyone who approaches know not to get too close. If the weather is bad, a cow knows which direction to lie to keep her baby warm and out of the wind and snow. And if mama and baby get separated, a cow knows which baby is hers, even though to me they all look alike!

As I watch the cows and calves, I'm reminded how much of mothering is instinctive. Before the arrival of our first child, before we even dream of becoming mothers, God prepares us. He puts the knowledge and strength and love in our hearts that will help us know how to hold our babies, how to love them, and how to care for them.

Yet mothering children is harder than mothering calves, and there's plenty to parenting that doesn't come from instinct! We are faced with so many questions and decisions. Despite my instincts, I'm thankful that I can learn from other moms who are in the same season as I am, and that I can get instruction from wonderful mentors who have already "been there and done that" in parenting. These close, trusted friends are guides in my life; women who will listen and not judge; moms who may not have all of the answers, but at least understand the questions.

Instinct and instruction . . . with these tools I think I'm ready for this mothering job!

~ Amy Gullion

no one like mom

WHEN GAIL ASKED ME to stay with her three little boys for the weekend, I agreed. At that time, Brad and I didn't have any children, but we had practiced with many other "loaner" kids. I listened to the bedtime routine and thought, *No problem.*

They ate dinner, took baths, and were ready for bed. They sported happy faces as I read the bedtime story. After the bedtime prayer, I said goodnight and stood to leave. Matthew stopped me with another request. "Mom always sings to us. Will you sing?"

I was delighted! I couldn't think of anything I was more prepared to do. I knew their mom could not carry a tune, and my years of voice training were sure to impress them. We decided on a couple of songs and I began. Something was wrong, however. I asked what it was, and Nathan ventured to comment. With his face all wrinkled up, he said, "You sound funny, not pretty like my mom sings it."

What a lesson! I have been reminded of it so often in

the years since that time. No one can do it like mom. No one can take our place.

When I was recently making plans to be away for the weekend, Josh, our ten-year-old, said, "Mom, we're fine while you are gone, but it's just not the same. It feels blank without you."

I chuckled at his choice of words, but he is right. As moms, we make a difference by giving who we are. Gail is a great mom, not because she has a great voice, but because she doesn't leave her boys feeling "blank."

What is it you'll give today?

~ Jeanette Hillman

a seemingly impossible task

DO YOU EVER HAVE THOSE MOMENTS (days, weeks, or even months) when you feel like this task of mothering is impossible? Are we really qualified to bring helpless infants into the world and in eighteen years train them to be caring, responsible, contributing members of society?

In the early months, we hear conflicting information about what's best for our children, and are told that somehow our right or wrong choices will either cause our babies to excel in every area of life or to never reach their full potential. What tremendous pressure to put on the shoulders of new, sleep-deprived, first-time parents! It is a wonder that any of us survive.

Then there are several years of determining nap schedules or no schedules, when to begin solid food, what kind of food, and when and how to potty train (I am convinced that my children trained themselves when they were ready, and I just provided the opportunity). Then come the decisions of preschool or no preschool; when should they learn to read. Should they go to public or private school, or should we homeschool? The lists go on, and we haven't even reached the teenage years yet. Is it possible to make all of the right choices, we worry—what if we miss one or two (or more)?

I absolutely love being a mom, but it is, without a doubt, the most difficult and challenging job I have ever had. My husband says he imagines my days with three boys to be like "herding cats" or "wrestling an alligator." This always makes me laugh, but I think they are good descriptions of the almost impossible tasks we face as mothers. And in the midst of it, I feel the weight of each decision as if it is life or death.

Sound familiar? We put too much pressure on ourselves and other mothers by trying to impose these unrealistic expectations. But thank God the task of mothering is really not impossible if we remember that he has given each mom her own unique gifts and abilities. We don't have to be perfect. It's okay for me to be me. And with God's help, I will not only survive these early mothering decisions, but I will raise three wonderful boys with their own gifts, abilities, and talents, and hopefully they will go on to do the same.

~ Toni Barsness

the difference a mom makes

AFTER PICKING UP THE TRAIL OF LAUNDRY and back-packs that led down the hall, I wondered if this "mom thing" really was making a difference for my kids. Am I doing something important?

And then I saw my daughter, Madeline, exuberantly pursuing her interest of the day. It made me think back to the special moments we share. . . .

When we're driving along, sometimes she'll slip her little hand into mine, sit back, smile, and be content to just "be with mom."

Or the afternoons when she just can't wait to talk about her incredible day.

Or, when a not-so-incredible day includes an "owie," a kiss from mom makes all the difference. "Do you still need a Band-aid?" "No, Mom, it's OK now."

Or when it's time to go to bed: "Will you tuck me in, Mommy?" Two minutes later, with the covers tucked snugly under her chin, she's sleeping peacefully—feeling safe and secure after a kiss, a hug, and a prayer from mom.

A simple touch from mom does make all the difference in the world.

I thank God for the part he has allowed me to have in her young life. The trail of laundry will eventually go away, but the difference I'm making in her life is eternal and long lasting. What a privilege it is to be a mom!

~ Michele Hall

silent appreciation

NOT TOO LONG AGO, my husband called me at work. He was at home with our kids, and he said he just called to apologize. When I asked him what for, his response nearly made me fall out of my chair.

A few weeks prior to his call, Kendall had changed shifts at work. He now worked in the evenings, allowing him to be home during the day with our preschooler, and to be there when the two older girls got home from school. He was determined to be the ultimate "Mr. Mom," making sure the house was picked up, the kids had a snack when they got home, and they were occupied when he went off to work.

On this particular day, he had worked especially hard and had cleaned the house from top to bottom, even the kids' room. I usually make them do it themselves, but he had gone the extra mile and made their beds, put their toys away, and cleaned virtually everything.

Then the girls came home from school.

They threw their backpacks on the couch, ripped their shoes off and pitched them on their bedroom floor, tossed their coats on their beds, and headed to the kitchen table to gobble down the chocolate chip cookies he had made for them, which were still warm and gooey from the oven. While eating their snack, they got crumbs all over the kitchen table, left their napkins in a wad, and plopped down to watch television—all without a word of thanks to their dad. (Sound familiar?)

He pretty much lost it. He ranted at them for being inconsiderate and ungrateful for his hard work and sent them to their room. Then he picked up the phone and called me.

He apologized for never expressing how grateful he was for all I did to keep our household running smoothly; for all I did to care for our family; and for putting up with them never saying thank you. He was apologizing for taking me for granted.

Guess what, mom? Mothering matters. Your family may not show you that they appreciate you, but they do, even if they don't know it themselves yet.

~ Susie Sims

"forevering"

HEY MOM—what you are doing? I mean right now. This second. Nothing? Not true! You're mothering.

Okay, you may be reading an email. But you're still mothering. In the next room, your baby sleeps. Outside in the yard, your son plays. Over at the daycare center, your daughter blows bubbles with a wand. And you sit at your computer, working, reading, writing, connecting . . . and still mothering.

Remember that mothering is as much who you are as what you do. It's part of your being, your personality, and your thinking, as much as it is part of your actions. Mothering isn't something we slip off our feet when we go to bed at night or leave behind when we drive away.

Mothering is "forevering." It's making a difference day in and day out in the lives of those who depend on us for their nourishment and their hope. Sure, it changes with the ages and stages of your little ones. But mothering is "forevering."

What are you doing now? You're mothering.

~ Elisa Morgan

my hero

GROWING UP, I remember having to write a school paper about my hero. It had to be someone brave, who gave of themselves to do important things to help others. Ahhhh, that was easy. Dad. My dad, a "Modern Day Warrior," was the perfect hero to write about. After all, he was a policeman; and not just any policeman, but the leader of the SWAT team. He was definitely my kind of hero.

However, I realize now I had another hero, closer to my life. As I look back, I see all the little things she did.

She faced numerous daycare instructors, teachers, coaches, and other parents to defend and sometimes apologize for her children. That is bravery.

She drove the long two-hour trip from Boise to Twin Falls, almost wetting her pants, because she was not about to stop at a rest stop and leave my sleeping baby brother alone in the car. That is giving of herself.

She took my laughing, giggling high school dance team to shop for new uniforms before the first big football game. That may not seem important to others, but to the eight of us, what she did was the most important thing.

In today's hustle and bustle, it is easy to put aside the significance of motherhood. But being a mom is being a hero and a true "Modern Day Warrior"! And I just want to say thank you to my mom, and every other mom who gives of herself for her children.

Although they may not recognize your heroism now, someday they will!

~ Rachel Ryan

part two

take time
for you

time away

RECENTLY, I had the opportunity to go away for several days. While I was gone, someone asked me if I felt guilty for being away for so long. I hesitated. I hadn't really thought about it before. But now that she mentioned it. . . .

The more I thought, the more I hated having to be gone. Would my parents, who were watching my three boys, remember that they had to leave the house at a certain time to make the bus? If they missed the bus, how would they get to school? And would my mom remember that RJ has "Show and Tell" on Tuesdays? Oh, and did they remember that Phillip needs help with his spelling words? And Josiah's glasses, did I remember to pack them?

It's not that my parents don't do a wonderful job of watching my children, but they're not me. How could I have been so selfish to leave? Why did I ever take this trip? The more I thought, the worse I felt. I grabbed my cell phone and called home, but just as my mom answered, the battery went dead.

After worrying all day, I finally got to check in with my mom that evening. Of course, the kids were fine and not in the least homesick. I began to relax and started enjoying my time away. I could go to the bathroom alone and not have to put the seat down first. I had an entire bed to myself! What luxury! I didn't have to worry about what was for dinner, and I actually had time to curl my hair each morning.

When the trip was over and I walked out of the train station, there they were . . . my boys and my husband. What a reunion!

And after I returned, I found that I was a better mom for having taken the time off. By taking the time to stop being "mommy" and "wife" and just being "Gretchen" for a while, I was refilled and I reconnected with myself. Without these times away, I realized that I wouldn't have anything left in me to give my children or my husband.

So do I feel guilty for taking time away from my kids? Not a bit! In fact, I'm looking forward to the next time I get to take a trip by myself . . . but I'll make sure my cell phone stays charged!

~ Gretchen Jenkins

getting real

LAST WEEKEND, I sat in a circle of women—girlfriends really—exchanging stories about our children and the challenges of mothering. It was almost like "Can you top this one?" One graphically described the kinds of sounds and words that come out of her young sons' mouths at the dinner table. Another confessed the struggles she feels in making choices as a working mother. Another described how she tried to control her anger recently when her son threw up in church after taking his first communion. (I about threw up myself, I laughed so hard at her descriptions.)

We laughed together, we prayed, we offered suggestions to each other. But more than that, we normalized the warps and woofs of our lives: the roller coaster ride between good and not-so-good moments; the mommy-guilt and unspoken longings and unrealistic expectations. We brought the highs and lows to a happy medium. We got real.

This week, as I bump along in the normal chaos of life, the memory of our time together is like a balm to my soul. As women, we offer so much to each other when we share ourselves. We create safe places to be real.

Ahhhh . . . girlfriend time is good.

~ Carol Kuykendall

home alone!

. . . .

RECENTLY, my husband, Pete, and I had something happen that hadn't occurred in over fifteen years: we had an empty nest for an entire night! Our three boys all had overnight plans somewhere besides home. An entire house with just the two of us! We decided to take advantage of the childless situation and have a romantic dinner at home.

The steaks were grilling, potatoes baking, vegetables sautéing, table set with the fine china, candles lit, wine poured—everything was perfectly timed and the mood was set. I turned on the CD player to start the romantic music. Just as we sat down, an unexpected (but very familiar) sound blasted out.

"Hi, I'm Kris, and welcome to an 'Adventure in Odyssey'!"

One of our boys had a story CD still in the player, and I had chosen the wrong track for our romantic music.

Pete and I laughed; even though the boys were gone, their presence was certainly felt. Then we changed the CD and went back to our own adventure together.

Carving out time to spend with your spouse (or if you're not married, friends and other adults) is part of parenting. If you haven't been alone together for a long time, try to find a way to make it happen. Find the time to rekindle your feelings for the man who shares your bed. Our children need to see us investing in our relationship; someday they too may be married.

~ Rochelle Nelson

date night

I'VE GOT MY SCHEDULE, my husband's schedule, and our three children's schedules lying here, all to be combined into one Master Family Calendar. It is amazing how quickly the time fills up with meetings, work, field trips, sports, community events, and church activities.

As I look over the upcoming weeks, I wonder, *What happened to date night?*

Several years ago, we had a speaker at MOPS talk about intimacy and the value of nurturing this quality in your marriage. I rose to the challenge. I came home, pulled out our Master Calendar, selected a day, and wrote my husband's name boldly on the square.

Several days passed before he noticed and questioned me as to why it was there. I explained what I learned at MOPS, how we as a couple needed to find time to be alone together. If everything and everyone else could earn a spot in my life, I told him, then he deserved my time as well; after all, he was the most important person to me. Our time alone together was valuable and significant.

He liked the idea, and after our first date night he would check every month to see when our next date was. I think it helped him sense his importance in my life, knowing that a special time was set aside just for us. It was challenging, and some months our night out turned into lunch between errands, but lately it has disappeared completely from our list of things to do.

I miss date night. I liked the positive effect it had on our marriage and family. I think it's time to place my husband's name boldly on our calendar once again.

~ Vicki Perry

what do you need?

· · · · · · · · · · · · · · · · · ·

MY MOM IS ABOUT TO CASH IN on her Christmas present—a night at a local bed and breakfast, just for her. She can read, relax, and let someone else worry about the cooking and the cleaning. Sounds simple enough, but it's a gift that almost didn't happen.

A few days before Christmas, my dad and I talked about what he should give her. We couldn't think of anything that she needed, and my parents don't have room for more stuff, anyway. So we started talking about "intangible" presents: tickets, travel, an experience of some kind. The bed and breakfast was actually my idea. I know how much I need a break sometimes, but I can't remember my mom ever going away by herself.

I'm the oldest child and my youngest sister is still in middle school, so my mom has been in the midst of daily mothering—meals, chauffeuring, toys, homework, discipline, laundry—for almost thirty years, in addition to working part-time, volunteering at church, and caring for a house, pets, her own mother, and of course, my dad.

The next day, I happened to be in the room when my dad told her, "Beth had an idea for you for Christmas, but I think you'd hate it." Uh-oh. "She wants me to send you away, all by yourself, overnight."

My mom raised an eyebrow. "Why would I hate that?"

He should have stopped. He should have seen "the look." But he didn't. He kept talking, "Why would you want to go away from the people you love? You can read or do whatever you want all day when Emily is at school and I'm at work. You have plenty of time for yourself."

Needless to say, by the time that conversation ended, my father was wrapping a gift certificate for a suite in a charming bed and breakfast.

I still don't think he understands why it's a good gift, but that's OK. He did the right thing in the end, and his blunder helped me remember an important truth: no one, not even your high school sweetheart whom you've been married to for thirty years, is a mind reader. Unless you tell them, even the people closest to you may not recognize when you're overwhelmed, tired, or at the end of your rope.

What do you need today, mom? A few hours away? Help with dinner or the housework? A listening ear? Say it. Ask for it. Use words. Don't just wait for someone to notice.

~ Beth Jusino

girlfriend time

THERE IS ONE THING I REALLY MISS about my single days: time for girlfriends. I love being married and I love being a mom, but the time and energy demanded by these primary relationships don't leave many opportunities for pursuing or maintaining deep relationships with my girlfriends.

My friends understand—most of them are moms in the same boat. By the time we work around nap schedules, work schedules, travel schedules, doctor appointments, and babysitters, we all collapse onto our respective sofas and decide that maybe a phone chat is the best we can do this month.

But frankly, not investing in friendships leaves a huge hole in my life. And so one of the adjustments I am determined to make this year is to spend more time, and have more fun, with my girlfriends. This will take some real effort on my part, especially in the dead of winter, when my instinct is to hibernate. But here are some of the ways I intend to get started:

Be intentional! Take the initiative to propose activities and get them on the calendar.

Start simple. Have coffee while the kids play.

Get creative with babysitting. If my group of friends

agrees to exchange babysitting, a few of us can get out at a time.

Have fun! Risk doing things that we rarely (or never!) get to do anymore.

Spend an afternoon browsing antique shops or art galleries.

Sign up together for an art or dance class.

Invite friends to give each other a "glamour makeover," and then go out to see a movie.

Arrange for my family to spend the night elsewhere, and host a slumber party or a "crop-till-we-drop" scrapbooking party.

Call the local day spa and see if we can get a group rate.

What about you, mom? How can you make girlfriend time more intentional this year?

~ Paula Brunswick

dinner play dates

MY BEST FRIEND, Anne, has three sons roughly the same ages as our three sons. Fortunately, when they were small they enjoyed playing together, so we often traded babysitting. I chuckle at calling it a "play date," which seems so innocent for the phenomenon of six little boys and one mommy spending a winter afternoon together in a tract home.

Our husbands both traveled frequently during the week, and winter nights dragged long after days spent with busy, housebound boys. So Anne and I hit upon a wonderfully uncomplicated weekly routine that went like this:

Anne called at 4:00 p.m. on Wednesday. "You busy tonight?"

"Nope."

"Bring the boys over at 5:30," she said. Rule Number One: No worrying what the house looks like. Hers was always more picked up than mine, but I got over it and so did she.

"I have a package of hot dogs, buns, some carrots, and chocolate chip ice cream," I offered. Rule Number Two: No cooking or going to the store. We just pooled leftovers.

Rule Number Three allowed me to wear the black sweat pants and turtleneck with holes at the elbows that I'd worn all day.

We would feed the boys, clean up the debris, and then the two of us would sit down to hot dogs at Anne's kitchen table, enjoying easy conversation as the boys played.

What a blessing is a friend to be easy with on long winter days and nights!

~ Beth Lagerborg

celebrating
your birthday

DO YOU LIKE BIRTHDAYS? I see them as the once-a-year gift of a day to celebrate uniqueness. Think of your children's birthdays. You often plan a party with a theme, or get a cake decorated in a way that honors who that child is, or maybe who he or she hopes to be. A soccer player? A ballerina? An animal lover?

What about your own birthday? Do you still see it as your special once-a-year opportunity to pause and consider your own uniqueness? Do you celebrate it in a way that honors who you are? We don't need to outgrow the tradition of seizing upon a birthday to honor a person's uniqueness—even our own!

My own birthday comes in the summer, and when our children were little, I started a tradition of taking some time for myself on my birthday, my own kind of midyear New Year's Eve. When I was home full time, I got a babysitter for part of the day. When I went back to work, I took a vacation day. Every year, I plan some time of stillness in the midst of busyness, maybe by a mountain stream or on the lawn of a nearby park. I talk to God about who he created me to be, and where I am in the process of becoming that person. I look back and look forward. It's my style of celebration, which my family honors because the birthday person at our house gets to "call it" on his or her birthday.

How will you celebrate your uniqueness on your birthday this year?

~ Carol Kuykendall

ponderosa pine beetles

THE SOUTHWESTERN CITY where I live is situated in a ponderosa pine forest. Over the past year, many of the ponderosas have turned brown and died.

I heard that the trees were being attacked by a beetle that was killing them. At first, I assumed this must be a new kind of invading pest that the trees did not have the right defenses to fight off. But as the situation worsened, the local paper reported that these beetles had always been around. Under normal conditions, when a beetle bores through the outer bark of a tree, the tree fights back by flooding the hole with sap. However, with the prolonged drought in our area, the ponderosas have become increasingly stressed and are unable to produce enough sap to fight the beetles.

I think moms are like these beautiful ponderosas. Under normal conditions, we are strong women, able to fight off illness and cope with difficult emotional and mental challenges. But with the enormous stress of mothering small children, we can become weakened and unable to conquer everyday problems.

Unlike the ponderosas, however, we can get what we need to maintain health. Regular exercise (even a fifteen-minute walk) and nutritious foods can make a huge difference in our outlook, as can doing something for ourselves like reading a book or the Bible or attending a MOPS meeting.

What are you doing to make sure the "mothering beetles" don't get you?

~ Paula Brunswick

part three

letting go
and second
chances

while making macaroni and cheese

· · · · · · · · · · · · · · · ·

THERE WE WERE, home as usual, yet something would be different about today! My third grader was at school, and my preschooler and I were tucked cozily inside our house, just the way I like it.

For lunch, like every other day since he was able to talk, my son ordered macaroni and cheese.

I asked, "Would you like cheese and crackers instead? Or, how about a picnic on the carpet with finger sandwiches?" I was trying to avoid the old cheesy standby. But he was persistent, and finally I obliged.

As I stirred the macaroni in boiling water, my thoughts began to drift. How many times had I made macaroni and cheese? My older son loves this stuff too, but now I pack him a sack lunch every day.

And then it hit me. My days of cooking macaroni and cheese for my preschooler will end! There in my kitchen, the steaming pot of water caught the tears I could not hold back. I knew "the ladder of letting go" was waiting, and it was time for me to take another step up toward my children's independence.

The letting go part of motherhood is a constant struggle for me. Sure, I know that God gave us these precious angels to care for while here on earth. Sure, I know they belong to him, but I have become attached!

My little guy will enter kindergarten this fall (still four months away). He is ready, excited, and hoping it comes fast. Me, I need those four months to cook him more macaroni and cheese!

~ Jami English

changes

THE VAN WAS QUIET as we drove home after a long day. Without warning, uncontrollable sobs erupted from my daughter, Hilary, in the backseat. We had just passed the Dollar Store, and there in the window it said "Going-Out-of-Business Sale." It was closing. Change was coming.

How could they do this to her? This was where Hilary and Daddy took their dates to spend her allowance. This was where she bought grandma's treasured Christmas present. This was where she was already planning to shop for my birthday. Her life would never be the same! Change was coming . . . and she didn't like it one bit.

She got the "I hate change gene" from her mom. I remember when the quaint ice cream parlor in our town closed. To this day, I still miss it. As I patronize other village eateries, I often suggest that they add soft serve ice cream to their menu, but there have been no takers yet.

As a mom, I find that I'm resistant to change in my children. Each passing birthday reminds me that change is coming. As my children moved from infancy to toddler years to preschool and beyond, I have yearned to freeze time. I keep telling them not to grow up, but they never comply with my request. Change keeps coming.

But I have learned through the changing seasons of parenting that while I may miss things about the past, the future holds new blessings. Each new wave of change pulls memories into the sea of the past while depositing new treasures on the shore of the present. My challenge as a mom is to embrace all that each new stage has to offer.

As for Hilary, she is learning to adjust to the thought of life without the Dollar Store. We are already speculating on what might go in its place. Who knows, maybe it will even be an ice cream parlor!

~ Sandy Murphy

letting go
• • • • • • • • • • • • • • • • • •

I LOVE SUMMER! This is the time of year when my boys and I get to do something we all love—swimming! We start out the swimming season with lessons at the pool. I love to catch them looking up at me with pride when they accomplish what the swim instructors ask them to do. I don't dare read a book because I might miss them looking to see if I am watching.

After the lessons comes the fun part: the pool opens to everyone, and we swim! A few days ago, as my youngest swam from the side of the pool to me and back, it hit me how independent and unafraid he was. I let him grab onto me whenever he needed to and let go whenever he was ready. He felt my confidence in him, so he felt safe in the water.

What a hard job being a mother is! Learning to let go and allow our children to develop fully is tough. We want to protect them from the hardships that life brings—from skinned knees to hurt feelings from those kids who seem to love to hurt someone else. But letting them experience some of these things shows our confidence in their abilities and allows them to stretch their wings and fly . . . or in RJ's case, to kick those legs and swim!

~ Gretchen Jenkins

cutting the cord

ONE RECENT AFTERNOON, my three-year-old daughter decided she would like to experience the birth process. Taking her beloved dolly, she strategically placed it under her shirt and, with arched back, strutted around the living room with pride. My curious five-year-old son ran into the room, ready to assist. In a manner of delivery that any woman would envy, Mackenzie simply pulled her baby out from under her T-shirt. No needles. No pain. No waiting. As she cradled the plastic bundle of joy in her arms, Justin grabbed the doll and shouted, "Wait! I've gotta cut the extension cord first!"

As I sat giggling, I realized that there is some truth to the idea that children have an "extension cord." During pregnancy, the umbilical cord carries nourishment and oxygen from the placenta to the baby. This connecting piece of tissue sustains a child's life. After children are born, they no longer require its assistance. Independently, they use what God has given them to take those nourishing breaths of life.

Like the umbilical cord before birth, moms give nourishment and direction to our children when they are small. We connect them to the world, guiding them in their choices and decisions. When our children do something great, we feel pride in their accomplishment. When they stray, it hurts us to the core, although we know that it is part of a child's growth process to independently make both good and bad decisions and learn from them.

Mom, take an opportunity today to "cut the extension cord" for a moment to see what your child does. By allowing our preschoolers to make small choices in our presence, we gain greater clarity in how they will make choices in our absence.

As the saying goes, "Give a man a fish, feed him for a day. Teach a man to fish, feed him for a lifetime."

~ Robyn Randall

ahhhh . . . perfection!

MY CHILDREN ARE ABSOLUTELY PERFECT. Little angels. They never fight with each other. They never sass their parents. They are always well behaved and loving. Even my thirteen-year-old daughter does not mind snuggling with her mom. They don't make messes around the house, and I always know where they are and what they are doing.

Of course, this is when they're asleep. A mom can have her fantasies, right? The real truth is that my children often act exactly the opposite when they're awake.

No one has perfect children. They are humans just like us, with their own idiosyncrasies, personality quirks, and attitudes. None of us are perfect moms, either. We all want to do our best to instill good values in our children and help them to grow up into healthy and well-balanced adults. But we struggle and we fail sometimes, and so do our kids.

When I look at my imperfect children, I am reminded of the way that God sees his imperfect child—me. I think God struggles with the same things I do as a parent: he wants me to grow a healthy faith and live a well-balanced life with plenty of time for a relationship with him. But he sees when I am not well behaved or loving. He sees when I make a mess.

And if he's still willing to give his child a chance, maybe I should put away my fantasies and give my children a second chance today too.

~ Susie Sims

soap bubbles
and forgiveness

A COUPLE OF WEEKS AGO, my bored teenage son and his buddies pulled a prank on one of their classmates—they poured soap in his backyard pond! Now, this was not just any classmate and not just any pond that they chose. It was one of the wealthiest families and largest ponds in our area. And to make matters worse, our families attend the same church.

Embarrassed, I kept asking myself, *What is a mother to*

do? Where did I go wrong? I thought I taught him the differ-
ence between right and wrong . . . or did I? Couldn't he see how
wrong his actions were?

While I drove him over to apologize to the family and
volunteer to clean up the mess, I shared many of these
thoughts with him, and not in a nice, loving way. I heard
the same words come from my mouth that I had heard
from my mother when I did dumb things as a kid. Things
like, "I thought you were smarter than that," and "Where
have I failed you?" and "I can't believe you did this!"

I don't like it when I sound like my mother. Yet I know
there will be many times when my children will disappoint
me, just as I disappointed my mother. And as their mom,
I will continue to love them unconditionally, even when
they embarrass me and make me angry. Why? Because
I am forgiven. Does Jesus stop loving me when I make
a mistake? Of course not! It doesn't matter what I have
done or how many mistakes I have made—he continues
to love me through it all.

So the next time your child does something that dis-
appoints you, stop, count to ten, and remember the un-
conditional love that Jesus shows us every day, and the
forgiveness he gives disappointed mothers when they say
nasty things to their children.

~ Patti Nelson

"that's ok, mom"

TODAY I GOOFED. My son, Brett, had to give a speech in school, and he chose to talk about "How to Swing a Golf Club." Now, students are not usually allowed to bring golf clubs to school, but Brett was given permission to bring in a real golf club for his speech as long as I drove him to school and picked him up at the end of the day.

This morning, I drove Brett to school and wished him luck with his speech. But this afternoon, I was working at the computer when the phone rang. It was the school secretary.

"Mrs. Reese, Brett is here in the office. He says you were going to pick him up today." Uh-oh, I looked at my watch—twenty minutes after school ended!

I rushed to school and found Brett sitting with his golf club. After apologizing to the secretary, I turned to Brett and said, "Oh, honey, I'm sorry. I forgot to watch the time. I'm sorry I wasn't here to pick you up."

Brett replied calmly, "That's OK, Mom." And that was it! No complaining, no reprimand, no lecture on "Don't let it happen again!" Just "That's OK, Mom." WOW. Forgiven, just like that.

I keep thinking about what Brett did. Am I that forgiving when my boys goof? Or do I end up giving them a hard time about their mistakes? I know I will make mistakes again and so will my boys. My prayer today is that I will remember how relieved I felt when I was forgiven so easily, and that I will return the love in the same way.

~ Sylvia Reese

how come I deserve that?

· · · · · · · · · · · · · · · · ·

SOMETIMES I THINK I must be the worst mother in the world. I am forgetful, often stressed out, and sometimes even lose it with my children.

For instance, my five-year-old is the baby of the family, so of course she thinks she rules the roost and likes me to cater to her every whim. Yesterday morning when I attempted to wake her up, she grunted at me, rolled over, and went back to sleep. By the time I finally got her out of bed, I was running late for work and was quite angry. Then she wanted me to get her clothes for her and help her get dressed, although she has been able to do this herself for quite some time. I ended up yelling at her by the time we rushed out the door.

But do you know what she did last night? She came into my room and gave me the biggest hug and kiss and said, "I am so lucky to have a mom as great as you!" Now, I KNOW I did not deserve that.

Being a mom is such a humbling experience. No matter how many mistakes we make, our children still love us—every day. No matter how badly we mess up, our children always forgive us, always have time to give us a hug and kiss goodnight, and still think that THEIR mom is the best. My children have taught me so much. They have taught me that it is never too late to say, "I'm sorry." They have taught me that hugs heal. They have taught me that I am worthy of their love. But most of all they have taught me that mothering matters.

~ Susie Sims

part four

loved
by God

baby birds

· · · · · · · · · · · · · · · · ·

ONE OF THE HIGHLIGHTS OF MY SUMMER has been watching the birds outside my window. Just outside my office is a nest. I watched for several days as mama bird picked a place for it, tucked safely in a bush, away from danger. She worked tirelessly to build it from twigs, leaves, and even little shreds of paper that she'd found. She wove the pieces together and used her body to round out the inside like a teacup.

Speckled eggs appeared in it within a few days, and just like any good parent, mama bird kept watch over her babies. When she wasn't in the nest, I could see her perched on a branch nearby. When other birds came near, she'd chirp wildly, warning them to get away.

The baby birds sit in the nest and do absolutely nothing (kind of like my kids some days!), confident that their mama will provide everything they need. When they hear her approaching, they simply throw their heads back, open their little mouths wide, and receive the good gift she's brought.

I want to be like that! Like the babies, there are some things we can't get for ourselves, and it is only through our dependence that our needs are met. Even moms have moments when we need to sit quietly and wait for God, our spiritual provider, to come and fill our souls with what we need.

So open your mouth, and your heart, wide today and see how you are filled!

~ Lori McCary

two minutes

ONE OF THE GREATEST LESSONS of my life was learned through a pregnancy test. The lesson was not in love or parenting, time management or self-discipline, although I learned those things too. In a new way, I understood the existence of God.

When I thought I might be pregnant with our first child, I knew I felt different. I wasn't at the point of nausea or bouts of crying for no reason. To this day, I can't explain what motivated me to take that test. I just felt different. And so I did, and I waited,

and waited,

and waited,

for the two minutes to reveal to me what I couldn't even begin to imagine. And in just two minutes, my life changed forever.

I was going to be a mom.

We were going to be parents.

Two minutes before, it was just me. Two minutes later, I knew there was an existence, a human growing inside of me. While no physical developments changed in those two minutes, my mind was convinced that I was pregnant because the test said there was a baby in there. My doctor confirmed it.

I couldn't see him,

I couldn't feel him, and

I couldn't talk to him.

Yet I believed that I was pregnant. I took their word for it. I accepted it by faith.

And suddenly, I had this window of understanding into my acceptance of God. Søren Kierkegaard said that "faith is holding onto uncertainties with passionate conviction." The writer of the book of Hebrews said, "Faith is being sure of what we hope for and certain of what we do not see" (11:1).

We learn those lessons of life at the most peculiar times.

~ Robyn Randall

bigger than mommy

MOM, I NEED YOU!"

With the speed of lightning, I was on my feet in the dark, not really waking up until I was halfway down the hall. "What's wrong, sweetheart? Did you have a bad dream?"

Our three-year-old croaked, "I don't feel so good."

I felt his forehead, pulled up the covers, and asked, "Does your throat hurt?"

"Uh-huh, and my tummy feels like it's going to be sick too."

I hurried to the medicine shelf, returning with a thermometer, Tylenol, decongestant, and a glass of water. I wondered if I should get the steamer. As I bustled around, I reassured him, "Mommy is going to take good care of you and get you all better."

That tiny, croaky voice said, "But Mom, what I really want is for you to ask God to make me better."

Oh, how quickly a little boy brought his all-grown-up mom to a halt. I want to believe that I can be everything my child needs. But the truth is that, in a way, I am no more than a child myself. While there are lots of needs I can meet, my little guy already knows there is someone bigger than mommy.

~ Lil Bowers

gifts from my father

MY FATHER WAS AN HONEST, hardworking man whose mission in life was to provide for his family. He started a business at twenty-one and worked until he died at sixty-three. On our birthdays, my father gave each of his children a silver dollar—or brand-new dollar bill, as we got older—for every year that we had lived. (Of course, he also immediately whisked the money away to put into a savings account.)

My father died in the spring, one month before my twenty-fifth birthday. When my mother cleaned out his dresser, in the top drawer she found an envelope containing twenty-five crisp one-dollar bills. On the front, the envelope read, "For Beth."

I saved one of those bills and keep it carefully folded in a wallet compartment where my boys won't find it. It reminds me of my father's love and provision for me. But as the years have passed, it also reminds me of my heavenly Father's love and provision for me.

No matter what I need, God has the provision ready. Not in the form I may think, and not necessarily at the time I demand it. But he gives me the very best—brand-new gifts, like the brand-new dollar bills from my father. This is what I've learned from two faithful fathers.

~ Beth Lagerborg

cast all your cares

WHETHER OUR CHILDREN ARE PRESCHOOLERS or college-age, all mothers worry about whether we are adequately preparing them to be independent, to stand firmly in what they believe.

I was reminded of this again last month, when our oldest daughter, Meagan, left for her second semester of college. When she first went away in August, I struggled with her being five hundred miles from me. I would wake up in the middle of the night, wondering and worrying. What if she needed me? What if something happened and I needed to get to her? Would she be able to stand strong in her faith with all the temptations of dorm life at a large university? Did I teach her everything I should have or could have? Who would watch out for her?

In the middle of this, though, I came across a Bible verse that offered a great deal of comfort. First Peter 5:7 states: "Cast all your anxiety on him because he cares for you." What a great comfort, indeed! I took the verse's advice and turned to God in prayer, asking him to take this worry from me.

Right away, I was filled with peace. I knew I didn't have to carry the burden of my daughter anymore. Everything I did as a parent up to this point had prepared my child for when she would leave home. With every story I had read her, every time we talked, and every time we sang, I planted seeds and nourished her soul. I have done what I can, but now her Father in heaven must carry her as she lives what has been planted in her heart.

What a joy it is now to wake up refreshed after a good night's sleep!

~ Patti Nelson

everyday miracles

LAST YEAR, MY FAMILY enjoyed a dream vacation to Hawaii. One afternoon, we visited the famous Black Sand Beach, where black volcanic rocks tossed by the churning waves digress to smooth "river" rocks and finely ground black sand. Having seen nothing like those waves before, my daughters were enamored with holding hands with their daddy and trying to withstand the force of the water.

A huge wave rolled in and easily toppled the girls, completely covering both of them. After their daddy helped them back to their feet, we realized a catastrophe: our eldest was missing her glasses! Her vision was so bad without them that she had left them on as she played in the waves.

We all began frantically searching for those glasses. Other vacationers enjoying the water learned of our dilemma and some began to search as well, but we all knew we were never going to see them again. Her thick, heavy glasses would sink right to the bottom and, even if we could find them in the waves and sand, the rocks would ruin them.

Our daughter was frantic, thinking that the rest of her vacation would be ruined. Trying to comfort her, I heard myself saying that the God of the universe, who created that massive ocean, knew exactly where those glasses were at that precise moment. And, if he chose to do so, he was the only one who could return them to us.

About forty-five minutes later, not really believing we would see the glasses again, my husband and I walked down the beach and talked about how we would replace her glasses. Suddenly, a huge wave rolled in, completely drenching our towels. As the water receded, on the sand at my husband's feet appeared Megan's glasses. They had a few scratches around the edges of the lenses and the frames had taken a beating, but she's been wearing them ever since!

Only God can explain how they made their way back to us. But that day, he taught me that everyday miracles do occur—if we're willing to ask for them.

~ Andrea Peterson

pictures in the sky
· · · · · · · · · · · · · · · ·

I WOULD BE WILLING to bet that before you became a mom, you had forgotten about the times your childhood self gazed into the heavens just to see what kind of pictures you could find there. I'm talking about those puffy white clouds you see so often in the spring and on those lazy days of summer.

The other day I was at the park with my children and they started saying, "I see a dog!" "I see a bunny!" "I see a three-headed dragon with floppy ears!" WHAT!? It took me a moment to figure out what in the world they were talking about. I turned my gaze to the clouds too, but all I saw were puffs of white, caused by the condensation of water as it evaporates.

Isn't it funny how we adults forget to notice the wonderful things around us that God has created? As I spend time outdoors with my children, I am learning again how to spot the pictures in the sky. It takes practice. We lose a bit of our imagination as we grow older. How wonderful when God gives us another chance, through our children, to be like children again.

Take a moment to notice the clouds as they roll along with the wind. And when you do see a three-headed dragon with floppy ears, remember who put him there, and that he loves you very much.

~ Susie Sims

part five

life's
irretrievable
moments

choosing what matters most

. . . .

How do I make the best choice about what to do? Do I sort, wash, and fold the clothes or take advantage of this blue-sky day and take the kids to the park to hunt for the first signs of spring? Do I get a babysitter and go with my friend who is scared about her doctor's appointment? Do I offer to be one of the mom-helpers on the preschool's field trip to the Children's Museum?

These kinds of questions pop up over and over during our years of mothering young children, and I never knew how to choose the right answer—until I heard a little phrase.

"Make the most of life's irretrievable moments," someone older and wiser told me. Since then, those seven simple words have helped me make choices about what matters most.

First, think about the meaning of "irretrievable moments." It means the moments that might not come around again—the ones that may happen only once. Mothering is filled with moments that keep coming back. If you miss one of them, don't worry, because it will come around again tomorrow. So you won't really miss it. Like unloading the dishwasher. Or sorting laundry.

But some may happen only once. Like taking advantage of the best spring day. Like helping a friend in need. Like going on a field trip. Those are the ones not to miss. Those are the ones to choose. Because those probably matter most.

~ Carol Kuykendall

invitation to a special moment

LAST WEEK I MADE A BATCH OF BAR COOKIES one evening, not for a meeting or an event, but just because. The way my family carried on, you would think I'd never made a cookie for them before that day.

My almost-sixteen-year-old son grabbed some cookies while I was reading email at the computer. He said, "Hey Mom, why don't you come sit with me while I have a cookie?" Wow—what an offer! I hurried to the dining room table. We didn't talk about anything in particular, and the moment probably meant more to me than to

Andrew. He's an extrovert and doesn't like to do anything alone, even eating a cookie.

That time at the dining room table reminded me that I never know in advance when I will get an invitation to those special mothering moments. Most don't come with flashing neon signs saying, "This is an important moment to spend with your child!" Rather, mothering is a collection of lots of little invitations and choices. So whether it's another game of Candy Land, reading a picture book for the nineteenth time, or sharing a cookie, make the most of your mothering invitations—they matter!

~ Carla Foote

making a difference for tomorrow

· · · · · · · · · · · · · · · ·

HURRY UP AND GROW" were words I said often when my kids were toddlers. If only they could walk, if only they could be out of diapers, if only they could talk, if only they could go to school, if only they could drive . . . I was excited to see them grow from one stage to the next, and curious to see what kind of people they would become.

Today, Danny is twenty-two, Allison is nineteen, and Scott is sixteen. Obviously, they have grown in stature, but how have their spirits grown?

Four years ago, when Danny was packing to go to college, I had one of those "mommy panic attacks." Had I taught him everything he needs to go off on his own? Had I taught any of my kids enough about God?

I began thinking back over the last few months, and as I remembered moments with each of my kids, the feeling of failure faded. When my father-in-law lost his battle to cancer, it was Scott, my youngest, who helped the rest of us let go when he said, "Maybe it is time for grandpa to go live with Jesus." And when our family dog died after being accidentally tied up by a troubled neighbor, my daughter, Allison, forgave him and said, "This will help him get the help he needs." And as Danny was packing for college, I saw him pack his Bible, which had been untouched on his shelf for awhile.

Where did these great moments come from? I began to think back to my own MOPS years. I read many books to the kids about God and his creation, I listened and sang along to tapes, and I lay on the ground gazing at the stars and watching the clouds turn into animals or funny-looking people. I learned the colors of a rainbow, acted out the Christmas story, prayed over bruised knees and fears of the dark, and helped them see others who were less fortunate.

These many years later, I'm realizing how many little teaching moments I had with my kids during those "hurry up and grow" years. And I know now that what I learned in MOPS was true: what I did in those days did make a difference in my kids' tomorrows.

~ Amy Gullion

moments of spiritual opportunity

MY EIGHT-YEAR-OLD SON experienced the loss of a dear friend one week before he experienced grief again, this time on a much bigger, less personal scale—over the September 11, 2001, terrorist attacks. These two events brought mom and son together for moments of "spiritual opportunity."

The night of our dear friend's funeral, my son lay in bed ready to say his prayers. I'll never forget the words he prayed.

Dear Jesus,

Thank you for taking care of my friend and making him happy again in heaven. Thank you for loving me too. And dear God, remember that question I asked you? When do I get to go?

Wow! As a mom it took me a minute to take it in. My son didn't exhibit tears of sadness or grief, only joy for our friend and anxiousness to go to heaven as well. It is in these brief, innocent moments that windows of opportunity open up to us as moms. I was able to talk with my son about how happy our friend must be and how wonderful it must be in heaven. My son told me about his version of heaven: fishing streams, doggy houses, streets of gold, and Jesus coming over to visit.

When the terrorist attacks on America occurred, my son and I again had "spiritual opportunity" moments to talk about the people who died and what that meant. He asked me questions I couldn't answer: "Mom, how many Christians are there in America? How many people who died in New York and in Washington, D.C., went to heaven?"

Have you had a spiritual opportunity lately with your child? Look for those special moments and expand your child's world!

~ Cyndi Bixler

mr. rogers's parenting present

I GREW UP WATCHING *Mister Rogers' Neighborhood*. There I learned that I was special, that even goldfish die, and that make-believe can be real. But Fred Rogers's most important lesson for me took place fifteen years later.

During my summer break from college, I worked as an intern at Family Communications Inc., the production company for *Mister Rogers' Neighborhood*. One afternoon as I was copying scripts, Fred himself stopped to copy a poem for a friend. I offered to do it for him, and he stayed while I did. After a little small talk, I gathered the courage to ask him the question that I'd been wondering about for months.

"Fred, I've watched you talk to celebrities and little kids. No matter who it is, you make them feel special about themselves. How do you do it?"

Fred thought for a moment. "I guess I always try to be present in the moment for that person. I try to focus on them and to not think about other things when we're together. I think I owe that to them."

From that time, I made a quiet promise to myself to practice being present in the moment in my life too. It was more difficult than I first thought, but still I try.

Sometimes the laundry waits an extra day or I don't get as much sleep as I would like. I doubt the Christmas cards will get sent this year. And I rejoice, because those are all extra moments that we can spend together as a family—reading a book, taking a walk, or just enjoying a snack together.

I find it's the tiny moments that mean the most to me. Like the day that each of our sons turned because he recognized his own name for the first time. Or every time one of them lets out a big belly laugh. I might have missed those moments if I allowed myself to be distracted by small unimportant things.

Is that what people mean when they say that they spend "quality time" with their children? I don't know. I just know what works for us.

And so, thanks to Mr. Rogers, I keep trying to be present in the moment. I owe that to them. I owe that to myself.

~ Dawn Lamuth-Higgins

make today wonderful

THERE IS ALWAYS a choice about the way you "do" life, even if there is no choice about your station (or situation) in life itself.

We tell ourselves that life is too short to spend our waking hours picking up toys we picked up an hour ago, having conversations with no one but a preschooler, or enduring yet another ear infection. We subconsciously believe that there is a picture-perfect life out there somewhere. Surely somebody has it.

The danger is that in our longing for that perfect place, we begin to focus on the future or the past. In that focus, we will miss the amazingly wonderful life available today, right now.

Hints for making today wonderful:

1. **Choose your attitude:** Being a mom of a preschooler wouldn't be high on some people's lists of career objectives, but you have been given the opportunity to change the world by your impact on the little ones in your care.

2. **Play:** Take time to have fun. It's energizing.

3. **Be present:** Engage fully in your circumstances—work or play.

4. **Make their day:** Figure out a way to make it a good day for those around you.

~ Jeanette Hillman

"perk me up" moments for mom

I JUST HAD ONE OF THOSE HARRIED DAYS . . . you know the kind—soccer game, team pictures, science project deadline, library books due, snack schedule duty, church activities. Mothering is definitely not for wimps! It takes energy, organization, and patience to keep up the demanding pace.

Oh, that word: patience. Ouch! There are too many moments when I am short on patience and long on impatience. Impatient for the game to get over, impatient to get to the next commitment, impatient in the long grocery line, or impatient waiting for my child. In those impatient moments, when my schedule takes me to the brink of exhaustion, I often find myself asking the question—does any of this really matter?

It is exactly at those times, when I want to check out of motherhood for a day, that God sends me a "perk me up" moment. I find it in the soap scum on the shower door, where my little boy has written, "I LOVE YOU MOM." I feel it when my child searches the house to hug me after I've loaded the snack cabinet and exclaim, "You're the best mom ever!" This week I was sick and run down, and my "perk me up" moment came when little fingers reached under the bathroom door to offer vitamin C tablets to help mommy feel better!

Look for those "perk me up" moments the next time you're at the brink. There's always something to remind you that mothering matters!

~ Cyndi Bixler

for such a time as this

I VIVIDLY REMEMBER DAYS when I would find myself wondering if my children were simply placed here to torture me. All I could see was spilled milk, splattered peas, and baby beds finger-painted with "diaper paint." On those days I lost sight of my hope and let my focus diffuse.

It was during one of these challenging days that I happened across the story of Queen Esther in the Bible. Mordecai, Esther's Jewish relative, had just informed her of a plot to kill the Jewish people. Mordecai asked Esther to speak to the king and save her people.

Esther was hesitant—afraid that the king would kill her.

She was living the good life. Why should she put herself through such a frightening ordeal?

You were chosen "for such a time as this" was Mordecai's simple response to Esther (Esther 4:14).

"Oh, yes," I said to myself, as I trudged through my daily routine of dirty diapers, dishes, and laundry. "I was chosen for such a time as this."

It was on an autumn day, months after the "bed finger-paint" episode, that my four-year-old daughter, Jessica, found a snail that she named Sally. All three of my children played with Sally all day. Even I loved Sally. Anything that held their attention that long could not be bad.

That night Jessica carefully tucked Sally into a plastic butter dish. None of us noticed when she placed the dish on the heater vent, thinking she should keep her new-found friend warm.

The next morning Jessica came running from the den crying, "Mommy! Mommy! Look at Sally!" Sally Snail was dried up and cracked in a way that reminded me of my face when it is time to wash off a facial.

Jessica was heartbroken. I sat down to comfort her, stroking her hair and holding her tightly. In between her heavy sobs and body spasms, Jessica hugged me tightly and whispered, "Mommy, I love you."

Suddenly, the rigors of motherhood did not hold a candle to this moment. This was what being a mother was all about. My focus and hope immediately returned.

I could almost hear Mordecai speaking softly in my ear: "You were chosen for such a time as this."

~ Lisa Moffitt

don't cry over spilled milk

As I STEPPED OUT OF THE CAR this week, my recycled grocery bag gave way, unleashing a gallon of milk. Showers of cold, white liquid smacked the car, my leg, and the driveway.

While I trudged inside for paper towels to clean up the mess, I thought about how long it had been since I'd mopped up spilled milk. When my four children were small, spilled milk was a daily occurrence. If milk wasn't spilled at breakfast, it splattered at lunch; if the table stayed dry at lunch, I put a roll of paper towels by my place setting at dinnertime to wipe up the inevitable spill. On the rare occasion that little hands didn't spill milk, my elbow would hit my own glass as I reached over to cut a toddler's green bean into four bite-sized pieces. During those early mothering years, I was convinced I would spend the rest of my life mopping up spilled milk. Then, without my even noticing, milk began staying in its assigned space, and the "big buy" pack of paper towels lasted longer than one week.

I can't truthfully say I miss mopping up spilled milk, but I do miss the little people responsible for the mess. I miss baby voices that lisped a thank you prayer, repeatedly told the same knock-knock jokes, and declared me the best cook in the world when I served their favorite boxed macaroni and cheese.

If you're mopping up spilled milk today, take a close look at the baby faces around your table, because neither spilled milk nor baby faces last forever.

~ Shelly Radic

part six

fun in
the sun

small waves and other childhood discoveries

THE SUN WAS SLOWLY SETTING IN THE DISTANCE. Although it wasn't as bright as it had been earlier, there was still plenty of light for one last romp on the beach. The waves rolled gently to the shore. Huge? Not anywhere close, but to my three small children, they were enormous!

My husband's parents live on a beach in Florida, so one year for spring break we were able to put aside the "to do" lists, the incessant demands of school, work, car pools, and lessons, and the "frost kissed" Denver highways, and head for the slower pace of vacation and sand and sunshine. I found myself on "kid duty," watching my daughter Madeline and her cousins running into the waves. Over and over again, they let "huge" waves rush over them and carry them to the shore on their little boogie boards.

Their joyful abandon took me back to another time—a time of innocence, when fear and schedules didn't get in the way of the freedom to explore and the joy of finding something new.

I once read that the start of something new brings the hope of something great. For our children, everything is new and wondrous, and the future constantly holds great things for them to discover. God is a father who loves them so much that he has created small things—a smooth piece of ocean glass, a dried-up sea star, a pearly looking shell, the waves on the beach—for them to enjoy.

And I was reminded that the same holds true for us moms: we will often find some of the greatest messages God has for us when we embrace discovery and pay attention to the small things happening around us.

~ Michele Hall

spring fever

I REMEMBER, AS A CHILD, looking out my bedroom window at about 8 or 9 p.m. Although I was in bed for the night, there was still daylight outside. I couldn't understand why I had to go to bed when it wasn't dark yet.

I remember the smells of that childhood bedroom and the yellow daisy bedspread. But most of all, I remember wanting to be outside to play in the grass or walk in the woods.

On those bright nights, I had spring fever. Even now, as

a mom, I get that same feeling. When the daylight lingers, I want to go outside and play.

It's not that I want to relive my youth; it's that my youth comes alive when I see my own children filled with spring fever. They wonder at rocks and collect the best to add to their ever-growing collection. (I still haven't figured out what to do with the half-ton of pebbles in Hannah's bedroom.)

They stare at the clouds and discover lions, walruses, and horses.

They collect sticks and pick flowers.

They make bouquets and give them to me with muddy hugs and kisses.

In spring, my children come alive. I can see their excitement and joy of life. How high does a swing really go? Can you build a castle out of mud? Does the wind really have a song?

Springtime motherhood has given me just a glimpse into how God must see us. After all, we are his children. Does he get excited at our wonderment? Does he smile when we discover something new about his creation? Or about ourselves?

Don't let your children be the only ones in your family with spring fever. Get outside. Enjoy the wonderment of creation. Join in the laughter and joy. Share the wonder of being a child.

After all, you are a child too . . . a child of God.

~ Trish Berg

summer surprises

SUMMERTIME MEANS THAT THINGS don't have to run quite like they do during the rest of the year. Summer is a mom's chance to do what seems impractical when there are so many other activities, a schedule to keep, and earlier bedtimes. It's the season to run in sprinklers, lie in hammocks, and catch fireflies after dark.

Summer inspires me to give my children memories they will cherish. So yesterday, I announced that all I would serve for lunch was banana splits.

My boys looked at me in disbelief. When I pulled out the ice cream and whipped cream and cherries, they were amazed. "Are we really going to have banana splits for lunch? We thought you were joking."

(I did require a banana and fresh strawberries on each creation—for nutritional purposes!)

I like to surprise my kids sometimes; after all, they don't know everything about who I am, just as I don't know everything about who they are. One of the joys of motherhood is finding out more about each other every day, and sometimes it takes banana splits to find out that mom is more flexible and fun than she often seems!

That's the thing about summer—you never know what we'll be doing tomorrow!

~ Sylvia Reese

summer fun

. . . .

SUMMER IS A WONDERFUL SEASON FOR CHILDREN. At least, it was for me. My brother and I spent our summers fishing and swimming at my grandparents' cottage on the Tobacco River. As long as the fish were big enough to keep, my grandma would clean and cook them for our lunch before we ran off again to swim the afternoon away. I still treasure those childhood memories, and I long to give my own children some special summertime memories.

Summer with children can be so much fun. Bike riding can be an adventure for your whole family to enjoy together. And your children will love to play outside way past bedtime one night, especially when it's still light outside. I have even let my boys go to bed dirty during the summer.

Spend time doing special activities together. You can avoid using the hot oven and still enjoy making treats with the kids by frosting graham crackers and adding sprinkles to the top. Use sidewalk chalk to draw silly pictures or practice ABCs, or color eggs months after Easter.

Whatever you do, make it your goal to enjoy your children this summer and have fun.

~ Eve Caldwell

backwards day

WE ARE ALL CONDITIONED to want life to be simpler and slower in the summer. Trouble is, for mothers of preschoolers, life with the kids still has all the daily challenges, even though your MOPS group and other activities may take a summer break.

To get out of the daily grind, declare a backwards day! My kids loved to put shirts on backwards, say goodbye instead of hello, ring the doorbell as they left the house, and see if they could walk around the block backwards! Try reading your child's favorite book backwards, and you will all collapse into giggles before you're done.

How about chicken fingers for breakfast and waffles for dinner? Sit under the table to eat. Have dessert first—the world won't end! Your preschoolers will embrace backwards day and they will think of more ways to mix up the day and add some laughter to life.

~ Carla Foote

to love and be loved

DURING THESE "LAZY" DAYS OF SUMMER it seems my many roles as a mother multiply: dietician, nurse, social activity coordinator, mediator . . . the list goes on and on. Each day brings new challenges as I try to keep up with three very different children, their schedules, and their "creative" ways of approaching each day!

Sometimes I forget why I'm doing it all. But I recently read the words of a young boy in New York under the picture he had painted of his mother: "Being a mother must be hard, but no matter how hard, mothers always help their children and a mother is loving to her children."

Isn't that what all the juggling is about? Providing that safe haven for our children where laughter is heard, tears are dried, hugs are freely given, and love abounds. We will always love our children in a way no one else can. And not only will we love them, we will experience at the same time a love from them that is beyond description.

My kids remind me of their love in unexpected ways—like today, when Madeline called because she wanted me to know that there was a strange stain on the kitchen counter, but she "worked really hard with Windex" to get it out before I came home!

Yes, mothering takes time and energy, and it can be draining and frustrating. But each day brings with it reminders of a great joy: kids who know they are loved beyond measure and who freely give that love back to us! As you continue the juggling act, enjoy each summer day and the unexpected surprises it brings.

~ Michele Hall

midsummer adjustment

HOLD EVERYTHING! It's time for a midsummer adjustment. By now you're aware that summer is upon us, full-blown, lazy (for some), and hot. Are the days hurling by without a sense that you've done some of those distinctly summer things that are fun? Fun not just for the rest of the family, but for you too?

What is it way back in your brain that means "summer"? For me, the essential summer experience is swimming on a hot day, lying on the wet pavement until the sun dries me to a crispy lethargy, and then diving back into the pool to start the cycle over again. Somehow, no matter how many family barbecues we enjoy or how many weekend trips we take to the mountains, it won't be summer until I've had that sort of day at a swimming pool.

You still have plenty of summer days before you. Stop and think what you need to do to feel you've had summer, and duly enjoy this special season of the year. Maybe it's something as simple as judiciously editing the family's summer calendar so you can add spontaneous activities like all sleeping in a tent in the backyard without having to be up and off early the next morning. Maybe you need to spend some naptimes in the backyard in the wading pool. May you savor whatever experience lets you enter the fall knowing you can move on to new ventures—you've had "summer"!

~ Beth Lagerborg

daisy chains

ONE SUMMER MORNING, a blissful childhood memory surfaced as I quietly sipped my morning tea: I used to take great joy in creating daisy chains. It's a painstaking process, gently forming a slit in the stem of each daisy, then threading the next daisy stem through the slit like a needle and thread. When finished, though, we had the thrill of donning our handiwork around our necks or as crowns upon our heads.

It was such a joyful memory of a carefree, safe, happy childhood that the next day I took the opportunity to share my somewhat limited skills with my daughter as we created a clover chain necklace (for some reason daisies are in limited supply here). As I slowly and carefully shared the craft process with her, I watched joy spread across her face in the form of a smile. When we finished, she gently placed her necklace about her neck and danced around like a fairy.

As I watched her play, I saw myself again as a carefree child, contented with the flowers of God's creation. And I remembered that it's most pleasant to stop, smell, and listen to the world God created as the summer memories unfold in his embrace.

~ Samantha Mulford-Phillips

part seven

overwhelmed?
asking for help

hitting the wall

. . . .

DO YOU EVER "HIT THE WALL" IN MOTHERING? You know, one of those moments when you reach the end of your energy and patience . . . and the end of yourself?

One mom I know reached that point when she discovered that the three-year-old she thought was quietly napping in his upstairs bedroom was actually quietly dabbling in paints she had used to stencil a border around the ceiling in her own bedroom. When she walked in on the child, he had artistically stenciled the paint onto her new bedspread, new carpet, and across the newly wallpapered room. Talk about hitting the wall!

For me, hitting the wall meant reaching the end of myself in the late afternoon, when hours of whining and bickering and "Mommy" this and "Mommy" that left me with nothing to give to them. And WHAM! I'd hit the wall.

But over the years I learned something. When I reached the end of myself, I had a choice—to wallow alone in my own self-pity or to reach beyond myself and ask for help. When I chose to reach out and seek help, I rediscovered my need for others and developed more meaningful relationships.

That's what the mom of the young painter did too. She called a friend. "Help!" she cried. "Please come get this child before I wring his neck!" And her friend came and took the child for a couple of hours while this mom calmed down and cleaned up as best she could.

When we hit the wall and reach the end of ourselves, we can reach beyond ourselves by asking for help. After all, God never intended for us to do mothering alone.

~ Carol Kuykendall

wearing too many hats

I DON'T KNOW ABOUT YOU, but I think we'd have fewer "bad hair days" if we weren't trying to wear so many hats.

Wearing too many hats is my specialty! I mean, who will do it if I don't? There are so many things to do, and they're all urgent and so important!

Or at least, they seemed to be, until a few years ago when my daughter, Sarah, made an observation. She said to me, "Mom, I never want to be like you! You're not very fun, and you're always upset about something."

I could hardly breathe. What was she saying? Or more, WHY was she saying it?

Sarah was right. I was trying so hard to do everything and give her everything; I was wearing so many hats that I had become an irritable, driven woman. In fact, I had been doing so many "good" things that I missed what was best. The pursuit of good had left little to be enjoyed, and doing what was good had become the enemy of doing what was best.

When I heard those short sentences from Sarah, I came to the end of who I was and what I knew. But what seemingly was the end has now become just the beginning of life. Saying no to very good things has allowed me to slow down and enjoy those around me. Taking off some of those hats makes for fewer "bad hair days" and a much more enjoyable mom.

~ Jeanette Hillman

i want out!

I WANT OUT! I WANT OUT!" Our toddler, Jacque, had mastered these words, and she was saying them in a loud, clear voice—in the middle of a full airplane at the height of the holiday season.

Been there or somewhere close? If your extended family lives far away, it's not unusual to round up the troops and go farther than "over the hill and through the woods" to grandma's house. And during those long trips, when you find yourself trapped with a screaming toddler, she's not the only one who "wants out"! All of a sudden, in the midst of what should be a time of excitement and expectation, we "want out" too.

Moms have plenty of opportunities to want out: days when the diaper pail is overflowing, the "to do" list is way too long, the deadlines are piling up, and life seems totally overwhelming—and there's no end in sight. All of a sudden, this "mom" role isn't very fun. How much easier if God would just "let me out" and let me have my way.

While Jacque was screaming and I felt like the eyes of all two hundred and fifty passengers were on me, how I wished I could just give her what she wanted: open the door and let her out of the plane. Of course, that wasn't possible. Instead, it was important to go through the process, help her deal with the realities of the situation, and take her through those first steps toward understanding "delayed gratification."

You may be "wanting out" right now, or you may find yourself "wanting out" a few days, weeks, or months from now. We all deal with it at different times. When you do, remember the plane, remember the process—and in hopeful anticipation, watch out for the lesson on the other side.

~ Michele Hall

bringing home cloe

WE HAVE A NEW RESIDENT in the Jusino household. Her name is Cloe, and she is a red-footed tortoise the size of my fist.

She originally belonged to my cousin, Sara, who bought Cloe with her first income tax refund five years ago. She has lovingly cared for her since then, but Sara's life is different now than when she was in high school. She is deep into the mother-of-preschoolers season: her daughter is two and a half and her son is just four months old. She thrives on being a mother and loves her life, but the strain of raising two children has begun to take its toll. A few weeks ago, I received a phone call.

"I can't do it. I can't take care of so many things," Sara began. I could hear Ashley chattering in the background and the baby starting to cry. "I probably can't give you one of my children, but could you at least take the tortoise? I keep forgetting to feed her, and yesterday Ashley tried to throw her like a baseball."

Of course I said yes and drove down a few days later to pick up tortoise, terrarium, instruction books, and supplies. We negotiated a "temporary custody"; Sara will probably take her back in a few years when the kids are older and life is a little more ordered (tortoises live for up to twenty-five years). For now, though, Cloe is settled into the warmest corner of my living room, where she can eat every day and watch the world in peace. And the last time I talked to Sara, she sounded more peaceful too. By recognizing her needs and asking for help, she made her life just a little bit easier to manage.

Look at your life today, mom. Is there any area where you can ask for help?

~ Beth Jusino

more than a teapot

WHEN I WAS A LITTLE GIRL, teatime was a special time, especially when I was sick. My mom would bring a "sick tray" up to my room with tea and toast. The teapot was a small, old, faded copper teapot with dents on one side from our outdoor tea parties. The teacup and saucer were dark green and child-sized. There was something about the warm tea in that little teacup that would heal whatever ailed me.

One winter many years later, my two-year-old came down with the flu. I was exhausted after days with little sleep and many hours spent cleaning up after a sick child and washing countless loads of bedding. I was at my wit's end, so I called my mom, who was hundreds of miles away. Hearing her comforting words and encouragement gave me strength as I took care of this little boy.

A few days later, a package came in the mail. Inside the

package was the little copper teapot. Memories of those special teatimes came flooding back to me in a rush of tears. Some warm tea from that little teapot was just what my son and I needed that afternoon, and that little teapot continues to remind me that I don't have to mother alone.

Mom, it's OK to ask for help when you're having one of those days, when you feel at the end of your rope. When you talk to someone who understands what you are going through, it can give you a new perspective on your day.

~ Amy Gullion

hanging on
· · · · · · · · · · · · · · · · ·

IF YOU WALKED PAST MY HOUSE LAST WEEKEND, you would have seen me hanging on to an upside-down umbrella, with my feet barely touching our deck. It was certainly not by choice.

I had actually been enjoying one of those rare moments when everyone was out of the house; I had an hour of total peace and quiet to look forward to. Ahhhh—to be alone!

The wind suddenly picked up, and I heard a strange noise. I walked outside and saw the pole of our HUGE market umbrella hanging from the roof! The wind had caught the open umbrella and started blowing it away. If the pole hadn't caught on our shingles, that umbrella would have been halfway to Kansas before I even noticed.

I did what seemed logical at the moment. I grabbed the open umbrella and held on for dear life as it tried to fly away. With my arms aching and my feet barely holding on to the ground, being alone didn't seem like such a great idea anymore! Where was everyone? I needed help!

With each burst of wind, I was reminded of my own weakness. At that moment, I was totally dependent upon God to calm the wind and send some help. He did; my son's friend appeared on the scene, grabbed a ladder, and together we pulled the umbrella off the roof. How grateful I was to not fly away like Mary Poppins!

As moms, we face new challenges daily. We may not have the strength to hang on one more minute—but God will never leave us hanging alone.

~ Michele Hall

seeking boredom
. . . .

As MY HUSBAND AND I drove our three-year-old daughter to gymnastics, he asked if I thought our parents and grandparents lived the same crazy, activity-packed lives that we live today. After some thought I decided that their children were in sports, went to birthday parties, and had to be taken to school, but unlike us, our parents didn't feel that their children HAD to be entertained every minute of the day.

Today, if my children say they're bored, I'm tempted to immediately find something to fill their time, like video games, television, or outside activities. My kids don't know how to be bored, and I don't know how to let them. But letting our children "learn" to be bored now, while they're young, can be an enormous benefit for their future.

How about us? Do we, as moms, know how to be bored? Between laundry, bills, groceries, working, helping at school, attending a Bible study or book club, trying to maintain friendships, and so on, when could we possibly be bored? I know that some of these tasks in my house are critical, and if I don't do them there will be five people who are hungry, naked, and living in the dark. But is everything critical? Can I simplify?

Instead of encouraging me to simplify when I feel overwhelmed, our society suggests I learn to cope, or if I can't, to take medication. While I believe that there are many people who have a real medical need for mood-altering prescriptions, I also believe that medication has become an "easy fix" in situations that may not need it.

It's time we start giving ourselves permission to be less than everything. I have made a commitment to look at my life and eliminate (or at least decrease) the things that are not critical. I will not constantly stress about the state of my house! I will not add more to my schedule than I can do without resembling a decapitated chicken! I will not make my children run from activity to activity! I cry "Uncle!" My hands are up!

Give yourself permission to let go of the extra pressures that are weighing you down and seek a little boredom today.

~ Heather Rzepiennik

no two babies are the same

FOUR YEARS AFTER THE BIRTH OF OUR FIRST CHILD, we decided to bring another wonderful life into this world. Our first daughter was pleasant and content; she made mothering easy. We were ready for baby number two, assuming all babies are the same.

Seconds after giving birth to another girl, I knew this baby was going to be different. She cried instantly, and to my surprise, she cried continuously for the next two years. This new baby challenged every fiber of my being. Unlike her sister, she was not pleasant, only minimally content, and she put my mothering skills to the test every day. I learned all babies are certainly not the same!

As I look back over the past ten years with my second child, I realize that I also learned about my need for help. I couldn't do this mothering thing alone. My husband is a trooper who showed much more patience than I when our baby cried. He drove her in the car or walked around and around the yard, house, or neighborhood to quiet her. A few years later, I needed my dearest friend to help me as I helped my daughter through a severe school phobia. My parents and in-laws have always been available when I needed someone to watch the kids or give me a break. Neighbors have kindly played with my children while I did housework or when I was sick.

Asking for help was not easy, but when that second child came around I recognized that my need for help was greater than my need to appear perfect. My children benefit more from my care when I have help than when I am tired or frustrated, trying to do it all alone.

After learning to ask for help and seeing how much that help improved our family, it's no wonder we decided we would like to have a third child. Of course, we also knew there was no way a new baby would be as challenging as our second. After all, no two babies are the same!

~ Vicki Perry

part eight

windows of opportunity

grandma's flowers

· · · · · · · · · · · · · · · · ·

A FEW DAYS BEFORE MOTHER'S DAY, I sat in front of my computer and surfed the Web, looking for the perfect gift to send my mom. My week had been busy and the holiday had snuck up on me, so I was in a last-minute shopping panic.

My five-year-old son, Tim, sat patiently beside me as I looked at books, jewelry, and other whimsical items. Finding nothing that struck my fancy, I decided to go back to the tried, true, and traditional Mother's Day gift—flowers. We began to look at roses, daisies, and little, fun bouquets.

I finally narrowed the choice down to yellow roses or the "springtime basket" and asked Tim which he thought was prettiest. He looked at both of them seriously for a minute and let out a big sigh. "Don't they have any dandelions?"

Surprised, I asked, "Do you want to send Grandma dandelions?" The weeds growing in the backyard hardly seemed an appropriate way to thank the woman who gave birth to me.

But as Tim nodded his head, I realized something: nothing I purchase will measure up to a gift from the heart of my child, and his weeds will come with more love than anything FTD offers.

I turned off my computer and headed out the back door with Tim to pick his grandma's Mother's Day gift, thanking God for the "teachable moment" he gave both of us.

~ Eve Caldwell

"mollycoddle"

MOLLYCODDLE"—what an old-fashioned term. The dictionary definition of *mollycoddle* is "to coddle/pamper with extreme indulgence."

I'm a proud grandmother of two, but in my earlier years of mothering, I was called a "helicopter mom." I hovered over my children to "help and protect" them. That was my role, or so I thought.

A few weeks ago, my daughter, Sue, was going to drop my four-year-old granddaughter, Megan, off at daycare. Megan, in the backseat, was trying unsuccessfully to zip up her jacket. The zipper wasn't cooperating, and Megan's frustration level was rising, as was her voice.

Sue, of course, was driving and unable to help her. The

whole episode lasted only ten minutes, with Megs crying and demanding assistance!

All of a sudden, Megan exclaimed, "I did it! Mom, I did it—all by myself!!!" What a confidence builder for a four-year-old. It just took restraint on Sue's part to allow Megs to test her skills.

There's the story of the man who watched a butterfly emerging from its cocoon. As he watched the butterfly struggling, he felt compassion and decided to help it to freedom by tearing open the cocoon.

What he didn't realize was this butterfly needed the struggling to strengthen his wings. By "helping," he made the butterfly a cripple who could not fly.

The word "mollycoddle" takes on new meaning now. Our role should not be to pamper or coddle excessively or to hover. We need to prepare them now for their lives tomorrow.

~ Reneé Wheeler

are we getting it?
· · · · · · · · · · · · · · · ·

I WAS DRIVING HOME WITH MY TEENAGE SON, Ethan, after doing some errands. Things had been more than bumpy in his life. His string of not-so-good choices had left him with not-so-fun consequences. I knew I had to let him endure these consequences, but they were so inconvenient—and painful—to me! My brain and heart were fried from worrying about him. Was he getting it?

Out of the blue, Ethan turned and looked at me. "Mom, I told my girlfriend's younger brother about my choices and what I'm learning. He was amazed, and it made him think about his own life. I never realized how much he looks up to me—and that what I do or don't do makes a difference in what he chooses for himself."

Of course my mouth went dry. But because Ethan is a teenage boy who doesn't like big reactions, I stared at the car in front of me and put on my best "This Is No Big Deal" mom mask. But inside—fireworks! He was getting it!

Ahhhh, for the blessings of consequences in our children's lives—and in our own, as well.

~ Elisa Morgan

kitchen investments

EVEN WITH THE AID OF BETTY CROCKER, my kitchen looked like it had been hit by a chocolate cyclone!

My son and I had just finished making brownies. He was doing his part of cleanup—taking the boxes to the recycling bin and licking the bowl—while I scrubbed away at the rest. It was so much effort to allow him to help, and I was grumbling because of the extra work. But as I cleaned, it dawned on me that in less than one hour, I'd taught baking skills, measuring and math, money management (I explained why we saved the coupon in the chocolate chips), recycling, hygiene, delayed gratification (no licking fingers or the bowl until we were all done), and thoughtfulness toward others. I also gave my son the opportunity to proudly announce, "I made the brownies," at dinner.

Not a bad return on an hour spent mothering in the kitchen.

~ Shelly Radic

 go, ben, go!

GO, BEN, GO!" the young mother on the side of the swimming pool yelled as she watched her five-year-old swim in his first heat of his first swim meet ever. As little Ben struggled to cross the length of the Olympic-sized pool, I watched his mother practically fall on all fours, trying desperately to encourage her son to make it all the way across and not give up. Ben inched his way across the pool, swimming for a while, stopping to rest, clinging to the lane rope for support, and then off he'd go again to swim a little farther.

Before long, other spectators, including me, joined in the chant. There was no way that Ben was going to win the race, but it didn't matter. "Go, Ben, go! Go, Ben, go!" It didn't matter that we didn't even know Ben or his mother. What mattered was a little boy trying with all his heart to accomplish something, and we felt compelled to encourage him to do it.

It was an extremely proud moment for Ben, his mother, and all of us as Ben reached the finish line and exited the pool. Cheers and shouts of congratulations came from all across the sidelines, not because Ben won the heat or was an accomplished swimmer, but because he never gave up. No matter how endless his race appeared or how tired his little body became, Ben never gave up! And neither did his mom, cheering from the sidelines.

This week, take Ben's example—and his mom's. Look for ways to challenge yourself and your children to dream big, work hard, and, most importantly, never give up.

"Let us not become weary in doing good, for at the proper time we will reap a harvest if we do not give up" (Gal. 6:9).

~ Sherry Caldwell

wanting the best for our children

As MOMS, WE WANT THE BEST FOR OUR CHILDREN, but sometimes we confuse "the best" with a cocoon that protects our children from any bad influences.

When my daughter, Joanna, was four, she was in a well-regarded preschool program. One evening at dinner she wanted to demonstrate the knowledge that she had gained at school. "I know what the 'S' word is," she said coyly.

Yikes, I thought, time to take her out of preschool; I was hoping we could protect her from cursing for a few more years! I calmly replied, "We don't use that word in our home, so you don't need to repeat it."

She restrained herself for a while, but finally blurted out, "The 'S' word is 'STUPID'!"

Trying to hide my reaction of relief and laughter, I replied, "That's right, and we don't use that word in our house. It's not nice to call someone stupid, and you don't need to use that word anymore."

Sometimes it is tempting to pull our children back into the cocoon to protect them from every bad influence. What is "the best" for our children? Perhaps it isn't staying in a cocoon, but having a safe place at home to deal with the bad words, bumps, and scrapes that they encounter along the way. Then our children can have a stronger foundation as they go a little farther out to learn and process more.

If my daughter had really learned a curse word at pre-school, I don't think I would have pulled her out of the school. Perhaps I would have spent a little more time in the classroom observing and helping. But the reality is that it would not be "the best" for her to stay in the cocoon. My job as a mom is to give her a foundation and confidence to make right choices outside the cocoon, as little by little, she grows and learns.

~ Carla Foote

wild raspberries

RASPBERRIES, WILD RASPBERRIES TO BE EXACT, were the "passion fruit" in my family when I was a child. My mother especially loved the sweet fruit, which only seemed to grow in the narrowest, steepest, craggiest mountain niches.

Mother—a proper southern lady—seemed transformed on our annual vacations to Colorado. While my dad drove up the mountain trails and we three little girls perched on the back of our open-air World War II vintage jeep, my nonathletic, safety-conscious mother peered over the edges of the narrow road in search of her treasure. We'd hear a loud "STOP!" and see her VAULT from the jeep, balance across a log, and capture the prize: wild raspberries.

Who was this woman? What passion could cause her to fling herself down a mountainside for such a small reward? I remember the joy and pleasure on her face as she returned to us with a handful of the elusive berries, the sweetest and most flavorful in the world!

Now that I'm a mom, I look for my mother's passions in my children. What do they love? What brings them joy? Have they learned to take risks, be courageous, experience joy, and care deeply and passionately about something? Have I shared my passions with them? Can I even remember what I am passionate about?

As a mom, one of my jobs is to help my children discover their passions, and then, when they've found them, I need to be willing to "stop the jeep" and watch them pursue the treasures that bring them joy.

~ Karen Parks

rise up and call me blessed?

· · · · · · · · · · · · · · · ·

YEARS AGO I ATTENDED A COURSE ON MOTHERING that was offered through my church. We examined the "Proverbs 31" mother from the Bible, the one who is so hard to emulate. As a young woman in the throes of raising two preschool daughters, I remember thinking it would NEVER be possible for my children to "rise up and call me blessed" as the passage indicates. What could I possibly be doing right? I felt so angry and tired and frustrated most of the time.

It wasn't until several years later (when my girls were no longer preschoolers) that God allowed me a quick taste of that fruit. We were driving along when the radio blared the evening news headlines, reporting that Elizabeth Dole had withdrawn from the race as a presidential hopeful. I began discussing my disappointment. I had been excited to see someone of her position, values, integrity, and gender as a contender for our country's Oval Office. And I must admit that as a woman, it was exciting to consider the prospect of the first female president.

My daughters' responses stunned me, though. My eldest asked me if I could now run for president. When I asked her why she would think I should, her response was simply, "Because, Mom, you make good decisions. Every time we have a problem, you help us think through all the options, then choose the best." Then her little sister piped in, "Yeah, and you're really organized too!"

Needless to say, this mother was at a loss for words. Never in my wildest dreams did it occur to me that my behaviors would have such an impact on my girls. They actually saw my personality traits and disciplines as leadership qualities to be utilized. I was definitely humbled and blessed!

So, mom, in the mundane, everyday necessities of mothering preschoolers, remember that each and every moment can be captured as teachable and can have a future impact.

~ Andrea Peterson

our new family member

AFTER TWO YEARS OF PRESSURE, I finally caved in and agreed to let my sons adopt a kitten. I'm a "cat person" anyway, so it seemed natural to expand our family with a furry addition. And after all, I told myself, it's for the boys.

Those first few days with a kitten were not too different than when we had a crawling baby. She was into everything! We watched where we walked, carefully filled her water and food dishes, intently eyed her litter box for signs of "life," and did plenty of snuggling. We also paid attention to where she was in relation to our older cat, who seemed to want to take her off somewhere to have a talk about "who's the boss."

As the days turned into weeks and weeks into months, I waited for my little boys to grow weary of being caretakers. But I can happily report that they still take great pride in caring for their cat. Before my eyes, they have turned into little "daddies" to this kitty.

As a mother, I do my best to lay the groundwork for

them to become responsible, caring, and loving people. There are certainly days when I wonder if any of these life lessons we teach are sinking in. Are my kids getting it? Today, I'm happy to say that they are. My new family member is showing me that the time I'm investing is paying off.

Look around today, mom. Can you see glimpses of the adult your child is growing up to be?

~ Jami English

part nine

christmas
memories

"being" rather than "doing"

DO YOU FIND YOURSELF trying to be the "energizer mommy," just going and going and going—cramming as much as you can into every minute of every day?

I do. As someone whose reality is juggling work and home life, I sometimes wonder why I try to provide a designer holiday squeezed into the reality of a McDonald's time frame! And cell phones, the Internet, and all those time-saving appliances just feed into my feelings of guilt if I don't get more done; after all, these were meant to save me time and keep me connected with my kids!

But when I take a minute to breathe, I'm reminded that no matter what the time of year, no matter how much I think needs to get done, I really need to experience "being" rather than just "doing." God wants me to receive his gentle gift of grace and live with abundance and joy, to enjoy each moment without constantly checking my "to-do" list.

I know the holidays are busy, no matter what. But this

year, remember the "art of waiting." When you're stuck in yet another line, or find yourself in major traffic, take a breather. Instead of feeling frustrated, impatient, and jittery, give your mind a break. Stop thinking about the next thing on your "to do" list. Instead, allow your mind to wander and "regroup." Think about the awe in your child's eyes as he sees the Christmas lights sparkle.

Enjoy the moment—you'll be glad you did.

~ Michele Hall

fear not

IN THESE DAYS OF TERRORIST THREATS and concerns, we moms face various fears. Fear of traveling during the holidays. Fear of aged parents, their health and their need for support. Fear of children becoming sick at just the wrong moment—or at all. Fear of the economy's unpredictable turns both up and down. Fear.

As I made my plans for Christmas this year, I wondered . . . Will we really all be together? Will my elderly relative still be alive by December 25? What gifts would be meaningful this year? What can I count on? What do I need to be willing to lay aside? Which of my concerns are real enough to actually validate fear as my response, and which are simple overreactions?

I think of Mary and Joseph, who moved through deeply

uncertain days of political unrest, economic trials, and personal turmoil two thousand years ago. Each was interrupted in their sleep by an angel with two strong words, "Fear not. . . ." Huh? If ever a young couple faced a crisis, Mary and Joseph did! Pregnant with the Son of God, a teenage girl engaged to a carpenter—I'd say such a moment qualified for fear! But the angel encouraged them both, "Fear not. . . ."

Mom, as you and I "give birth" to Christmas around us this year, let's pay attention to the condition of our hearts. Are we fearful? For what reason? We have an example in the parents of the first Christmas ever, who faced and endured a season of incredible uncertainty with grace and courage. Their reaction to their days guides us through our own moments of need. Fear not. . . .

~ Elisa Morgan

christmas traditions
. . . .

SEVERAL TIMES IN THE PAST WEEK, people have asked me about my family's "Christmas traditions." It's a fair question—this will be the first year my husband travels two thousand miles with me to spend Christmas with my family, and he should know what he's in for. But I'm never sure how to answer.

After all, what is a tradition?

Is it a tradition to go to a candlelight church service on

Christmas Eve? To take turns opening presents on Christmas morning? To travel to see grandparents and aunts and uncles on Christmas night?

Those are all traditions in the, well, traditional sense of the word. But as I look back at the things I want Eric to understand, those aren't what come to mind. The moments and rituals I've hung on to are more unique.

Like the way we make Christmas cookies. One night, after the dinner dishes are done, my mother and sister and I mix, melt, roll, shape, and eat as much dough as possible. Instead of Christmas carols or other "traditional" music, though, my flower-child mother insists on baking to the tunes of Bob Dylan. To this day, the smell of warm cookies reminds me of dancing around the kitchen with Emily when she was just a baby, singing "Times They Are A-Changin'" while stirring chocolate as it melted.

Or maybe one of our traditions is the way that my mom and I Christmas shop. For her, it's more important to get me what I want than to surprise me, so we always set aside a day before Christmas when we leave husbands and fathers and children at home and go shopping, just us. I pick out what I like, and she buys. The drawback to this system is that I often end up wrapping my own presents, and there aren't many surprises for me under the tree, but our time together in the middle of all the busyness seems like a present in itself.

What are the Christmas traditions you remember, mom? And what will your children look back on years from now?

Don't be afraid to do something original—whoever said that Christmas traditions need to be traditional?

~ Beth Jusino

'tis the season

AS I ROUND THE BEND TOWARD HOME, I'm blinded by the brilliant glow enveloping our home. My husband has been hanging Christmas lights.

Mind you, he's not finished. But so far Alex has strung strands of tiny multicolored chasers along the fence, "blankets" of colored lights on the front shrubbery, large multicolored bulbs along the front porch, huge red and green balls (last summer's garage sale find) from the evergreen tree, icicles from the eaves, and a Rudolph head with red bulb nose atop the mailbox. Nativity figures cut from plywood are tucked in the front flower bed. The wooden star of Bethlehem strung from the aspen tree boasts a whole string of white lights peeking through holes drilled into the wood. Our oldest son calls it "Mary, Joseph, and baby Jesus in Las Vegas."

But our youngest son is my husband's overgrown elf, and together the two of them are incorrigible. I used to intercept them each year, before they began this annual process, to suggest they start with a plan. But they have a plan: more is better.

What to do? Finally, I had a brilliant idea. "Okay, you guys," I said. "I'll make you a deal. You can do whatever you want with the outdoor lights (as if they weren't already), and I'll be in charge of the indoor decorations." They agreed, and I decided to be satisfied with halting the inevitable inward progression.

We all have to give in sometimes. And it's not so hard, really, especially when it gives my husband and son such satisfaction. Each night before bed, Alex walks across the street and looks back at the house, admiring the cheerful glow. When he comes in, I make sure the lights are turned off for the night. Our season is truly merry and bright!

~ Beth Lagerborg

precious gifts
· · · · · · · · · · · · · · · · · ·

THIS SEASON OF GIFT GIVING and receiving always reminds me of an experience I had with a wedding gift nineteen years ago.

Just as many engaged couples do, my then-fiancé and I selected patterns for china and crystal, registering at the local major department stores before our wedding. After the honeymoon, I began to settle in to married life and to inventory the gifts we had received (only two toasters!). I noticed that we had received only two crystal goblets in the style we selected, so I decided to return them (beautiful, but pricey) and exchange them for a full set of less expensive glasses. I carefully placed the two goblets in a bag and prepared for a trip to the department store. As I stopped to lock the front door of my house, the bag slipped from my hand and crashed to the porch floor. Only one of the goblets survived the ordeal.

I stood there for a while on my front porch, pondering what had just happened. A moment ago, I had two beautiful, precious crystal goblets. Now one had become a pile of glass shards with absolutely no value. In an instant, what had been precious was reduced to rubble.

I thought about the other gifts I received and the physical possessions we owned. And while I was grateful for my many things, in that instant I realized that they too could be snatched away. As I looked at the broken glass, I began to see more clearly that I had better hold tightest to things that endure.

This Christmas, enjoy "the fluff and the stuff" of gift giving and receiving, but cling more dearly to what will last. Look to eternity and the precious baby born in a rustic manger. His value truly lasts forever!

~ Debbie Anway

my perfect dream world

I HAD CHRISTMAS PLANNED down to the last detail! I had worked hard for at least a month to make this the most perfect Christmas ever. My family had even come from out of town to celebrate with us. We decided to enjoy a nice Christmas Eve dinner and then go to the candlelight service at our church together. Tonight would be extra special because Ryan, my eight-year-old son, would celebrate his first communion since he had accepted Christ.

Ryan stuffed himself full of macaroni and cheese and chocolate milk (an unlikely menu for Christmas Eve, but it *is* a family favorite, so. . . .). We dressed in our Christmas best and headed off to celebrate Christ's birth together. Life could not have been more perfect!

The service was wonderful! When the pastor finished his message, we filed to the front of the church to celebrate communion. Ryan tore a piece of bread from the loaf and smiled proudly at me. Then he dipped it in the wine (aka grape juice) and popped it into his mouth. I beamed with pride as we headed back to our seats, and then I turned to congratulate him.

Ryan had a terrible look on his face that I recognized far too well! Since he had been a baby, he'd had a gag reflex like none I'd seen before, especially if the texture of something was not just right. Obviously that soggy, grape-juice-soaked piece of communion bread was not sitting well with him! I knew what was coming! I grabbed him and headed for the nearest exit and, between my gritted teeth, repeatedly ordered him to "Swallow . . . NOW!"

Just as we approached the curtains that surrounded our makeshift church, Ryan vomited the macaroni and cheese, the chocolate milk, and his first piece of communion bread dipped in grape juice EVERYWHERE. It covered my new Christmas sweater. It was in my shoes. It was slung across the floor. And to my absolute horror, macaroni noodles even clung to the navy blue curtains! I was stunned and so angry that I even surprised myself. My eight-year-old son stood staring at me in disbelief while I had the biggest temper tantrum of my life! I stomped my feet, I waved my fists in the air, and I angrily shouted things at him I had promised myself I'd never say! On the other side of the curtains, the worshipers were lifting their candles toward heaven and singing, "Silent night, holy night, All is calm, all is bright. . . ." Yeah, right!

I was anything but calm! Ryan's overactive gag reflex had ruined my picture-perfect, Christmas Eve dream world, and I wasn't handling my disappointment well at all! Because of the unbearable odor surrounding both of us, we would have to cancel our plans to see the Christmas lights and get home to change clothes instead.

The ride home was tense and quiet. My tender-hearted eight-year-old finally piped up from the back seat. "I'm sorry for ruining everything, Mommy."

I felt humiliated! I knew I was the one who needed to apologize. He hadn't ruined everything—I had! My unrealistic expectations had gotten the best of me again, and I had allowed my disappointment to spill over onto a little boy who had no idea how disgusting soggy, grape-juice-soaked bread could be!

How many times have my unmet expectations and disappointments kept me from seeing the joy and meaning behind our celebrations? Life will never be that picture-perfect dream world I had imagined. Christmas Eve was a perfect reminder of that! But I am so grateful that God sent his perfect Son to save this imperfect mom! Aren't you?

~ Lori McCary

the joy of christmas

I RECENTLY READ AN ARTICLE ABOUT JOY. The writer was asked what he did for fun, but he chose to answer instead what he did that brought him joy. After all, he said, fun lasts for the moment you are involved in an activity. Joy is deeper; it lingers longer and satisfies more.

Do I want my children to remember Christmas as a fun time? Of course I do, but I want this season to be remembered for more than that. I want Christmas to be about the joy that shines through and lasts.

In the hustle and bustle of the holidays, it is far too

easy to focus on the gifts and material things. Presents are fun, and they can make us happy, but our family finds joy in giving more than receiving. For the past few years, we have filled Operation Christmas Child boxes for children in need and participated in the Angel Tree program, choosing a child who is the same age as one of our kids and providing a gift requested by the child's incarcerated parent. Years that we didn't have the resources to provide gifts, we made extra efforts to give of ourselves in acts of service.

I believe my children find joy in these simple acts of giving. I know that I find joy in watching them focus on others. Even when they were very young, they understood the spirit of giving that came with choosing presents for less fortunate children.

May your family discover joy this Christmas!

~ Chris Ulshoffer

part ten

the precious and the important

the precious
and the important

I LOVE LIVING ON THE FRONT RANGE of the Rocky Mountains. The purple hues of the mountains against the blue Colorado sky are unbelievably beautiful. But one afternoon not so long ago, the mountains took on an orange glow. The sky turned gray with ash as a wildfire climbed the peaks and moved toward our neighborhood. We watched and waited, monitoring the mandatory and voluntary evacuations. The sun had set, but the fire outside was brightening the evening sky when that invisible "danger line" moved within two miles of our home.

As the flames grew closer, the possibility of having to leave our home became real. With only a car and a van to load, we had to decide what was important enough to take and what to leave behind. We packed some clothes and sleeping bags. We gathered the important paperwork and walked through the house making lists. We separated the things we wanted to take into two categories—"precious" and "important."

My grandmother's nativity set was precious. I had watched her meticulously paint each piece when I was a child. My husband's computer was important. It holds many things that we would have a hard time replacing. Our photos went on the "precious" list, as they show a family history that is ours alone. Schoolbooks and band instruments were "important."

As we completed our lists and sat down together to make the final decisions, it struck me that everything on the list was really just a "thing." Sure, they were precious or important, but they were still just things. What were really precious and important were the people sitting around me. The things might be missed, and some could not be replaced, but they were still only things.

The winds blowing over the mountains that night swirled, and the fire turned back into itself before it crested the peak. We were not forced to evacuate, but that lesson burned deep into my soul. I should never let the precious and important things get in the way of loving the precious and important people in my life.

~ Charlotte Packard

time

"TIME" IS A WORD I THROW AROUND A LOT. I need "time" for myself. I need "time" for my children. I need "time" for my husband. I should spend "time" on housework.

But what does time really offer? I think time is a gift that we give. A mother's time well spent can encourage a child's soul. Children love the time that mom spends reading to them or listening to them. When my oldest daughter was a preschooler, our favorite thing to do together was coloring. We could spend hours working on pictures while we talked. I confess that the housework was not always done to perfection, but my daughter and I had great times together. Today I look back on those memories and the time we spent as irreplaceable, because even now that she is older, she still loves to sit and talk with me.

If time is an investment in something, or better yet, in someone, who do you need to spend time with today? Maybe you need to take time for yourself, or spend some with a child, your spouse, or a special friend. Often, time is the answer for the encouragement we need—time to talk, listen, play together, and even work together. Tasks done together are more fun than when done alone.

What do you think of when you hear the word "time"?

~ Chris Ulshoffer

rise above it!

· · · · · · · · · · · · · · · · · ·

I LOVE TO FLY ON AIRPLANES. I love soaring high above the earth, looking down at the tiny houses, cars, fields, and trees. I know that I came from "down there" just a few minutes ago, but when I look at it from so far away, everything changes.

As a mom, I need to remember to step back and get that "airplane perspective" on some other situations. When I am in the midst of my kids' petty arguments ("She looked at me!"), or when I'm feeling that I will never clean the house faster than my kids mess it up, those situations seem to swallow me up. Those are the times I need to take a step back, get some perspective, and rise above it.

So many aspects of a mother of preschoolers' life are urgent that it can sometimes be difficult to focus on the important. When you are in the midst of a storm, or trial, or potty training, it may seem to engulf you. Try to pull yourself away from the immediate situation and ask yourself, "Will I remember this in five years?" What is the big picture perspective of this situation?

Next time you are in the midst of a struggle, try taking an imaginary flight (pick the window seat, of course) and fly high enough to get up above the clouds into the sunshine!

~ Debbie Anway

living today

SOMETIMES IT FEELS LIKE MY LIFE IS ON HOLD. It's like I'm just getting through today, waiting for some day in the future when, in my limited experience, somehow life will be better. How many times have I said to myself, "If only we had more money, then I could. . . ." Or, "If only I had more time, then I could. . . ." Or, "If only the kids were older, then I could. . . ." Perhaps you've had some of these same thoughts.

Three years ago, God used an event in my life to shape my perspective and to teach me about living in the present without feeling like life is on hold. I went through treatment for breast cancer. There is no question that this experience gave me an eternal perspective as to what is ultimately important in life—my relationships with God, my husband, children, and friends. But the unexpected blessing of the experience was how it also provided me with a perspective as to how important it is to live today to the fullest, so that life is not put on hold. If we really want to move to a new home or spend more time with aging parents or travel (taking the children with us), then we need to plan (within our resources) to do it sooner rather than later.

As mothers of preschoolers, I think we really do have a tendency to put off living today for the sake of tomorrow.

May we truly experience the gift of each day and live it to the fullest!

~ Janis Kugler

thirty seconds of time

I WAS READING AT MY DESK ONE EVENING when our young daughter, Amber, came up and stood at my side. After a few seconds, she said in a small voice, "Mom, I need a hug."

I smiled, reached over, put my arm around her, and gave her a quick squeeze. But my eyes and attention were still focused on what I was reading.

She flitted out of the room but came back two minutes later. "Mom, I need a hug." So the same hug was repeated, and off she went again.

A couple of minutes passed and there she stood again, "Mom, I need a hug, but this time with both arms." I laid down my book, put both arms around her, and gave her a tight, breathless hug, with several butterfly kisses thrown in.

When I asked her why she needed both arms she said, "Oh, Mom, two arms feel better!"

Why did two arms feel better? Amber knew that at that moment my full, undivided attention was on her. She was not competing with my book or anything else I was thinking about. She had all of me for one brief moment in time.

Amber is now married and expecting her first child, but to this day I still remember that hug and those little arms around my neck. Full, undivided attention does not have to be a planned hour of activity. Sometimes it is thirty seconds of butterfly kisses and two arms.

~ Becky Eims-Hinebaugh

walking around the block

WHAT A HURRIED CULTURE WE LIVE IN! Today, instead of getting some of your "to-do" list done, give yourself a little time with your preschoolers and look at the world through their eyes.

When I had a toddler, we had a little ritual of walking around the block after lunch and before naptime. Sometimes I would get impatient and want to walk at my pace. Do you know how long it can take a toddler to walk around the block? Every stick, rock, bug, and cigarette butt is so interesting.

Some of the sticks and rocks would come home with us as treasures—in fact, my now ten-year-old daughter still collects sticks and rocks on outings.

So take a break and go at your children's pace. Even if they aren't walking, just lay on a blanket with them and look around. You may find some treasures!

~ Carla Foote

perspective

· · · · · · · · · · · · · · · · · · · ·

IT'S A BIGGER ADJUSTMENT THAN I EVER IMAGINED!"
said my friend, a forty-something, first-time mother who
had just adopted her daughter from China. "But of course,
I wouldn't change it for anything."

Isn't that exactly how we feel as moms? No one or
no experience can adequately prepare us for the task of
mothering, a 24/7 responsibility that, even with the most
helpful of husbands, primarily falls to us. We're likely to be
the one to find the sitter every time we leave the house.
We're likely to be the one who puts the children to bed.
We're really likely to be the one who wakes up in the
middle of the night when a child is sick. And sometimes,
we're likely to be the one who feels taken advantage of,
regretting our loss of freedom.

But really, would we want it any other way? Let someone else be the one to find the sitter or put the children to
bed or wake up with them in the night, and we feel "de-
prived"—our natural mothering instincts tell us we should
be the one to most often meet the needs of our children.

It all boils down to perspective, and how ours changed
when we became mothers. As Elisa Morgan and Carol
Kuykendall share in *What Every Mom Needs*, perspective is
"the ability to stand between yesterday and tomorrow and
understand how today fits." Our mothering perspective

tells us that it's okay to put a bit of ourselves on a shelf for a while, because during this season, our mothering is making a difference in the world of tomorrow. When we drop everything to hold our babies while they are sick or disregard the clutter to read to our toddlers, it's our mothering perspective that tells us we've chosen well.

Yes, mothering is an awesome, time-consuming responsibility, and we wouldn't change it for anything. That's the perspective we need to thrive in this season of life.

~ Janis Kugler

"warm fuzzies" of motherhood

TODAY, TWO OF MY CHILDREN are cleaning our house from top to bottom. Before you get too envious, let me assure you that they are not doing this by choice. Last night, they kept me awake until after 1:00 a.m., laughing and talking loudly, in spite of my repeated requests (OK, demands) that they be quiet and go to sleep. They decided that since school is out for the summer, they could stay up as late as they wanted and sleep late in the morning. WRONG! I dragged both girls out of bed at 6:00 a.m. and presented them with a long list of chores. Score one point for mom!

Because I am angry today with my own children, I really struggled with what I could offer you. But in my moment of frustration, it occurred to me that I may need to be reminded of some of the "warm fuzzies" that make motherhood such a fulfilling job overall. So with that in mind, I ask you to ponder with me some of the things that fill our hearts with joy.

The wide-mouthed, toothless grins of an infant who smiles because you walked into the room.

The fistful of dandelions presented by a toddler who wanted you to know that she loves you.

The mural painted on the wall with crayons from the preschooler who wanted to help you with home decorating.

The hugs that come seemingly out of nowhere—just because.

Bedtime prayers from a small child who never forgets to thank God for mommy.

The great "belly laugh" that all young children seem to have.

Holding a child while he sleeps, because you can't bear to put him down.

Snuggling up to read a book on a gray, rainy day.

There, I feel much better. Do you?

~ Susie Sims

contributors

Debbie Anway was involved with MOPS for sixteen years, including as an area coordinator. She and her husband, Kevin, have five kids, four of them teenagers!

Toni Barsness worked as a telecommunications engineer before becoming the mother of three boys. "Becoming a mom changed my life. I love it and want to encourage other moms, especially during those exhausting preschool years."

Patricia E. Berg has published several articles and inspirational messages for ministries like MOPS International and is currently working on publishing her first book. Trish and her husband, Michael, live on a two-hundred-acre polled Hereford family farm in the heart of Ohio, near Amish country. She is the mother of four children and a part-time college professor.

Cyndi Bixler is the executive assistant to the president of MOPS International. Off hours, she is involved in her community teaching single parenting classes and in her church's divorce recovery ministry. A graduate of Oklahoma Baptist University, Cyndi has a degree in education and teaches piano. She lives in Littleton, Colorado, with her two children.

Lil Bowers has a lifelong ministry to children and parents, having served as director of children's ministry and the director of child development centers for several churches in the southeast. Currently Lil is MOPS International eastern regional coordinator. She and her husband live in Atlanta, Georgia, and enjoy visiting their three grown sons and their families.

Paula Brunswick lives with her husband and two children in Flagstaff, Arizona. Although her children are no longer preschoolers, she enjoys giving back to MOPS by serving as an area coordinator.

Eve Caldwell lives in Grand Blanc, Michigan, where she has been involved in MOPS leadership for fourteen years. She is the mother of four boys.

Sherry Caldwell serves as an area coordinator for MOPS International and provides administrative services for Discover the Joy! A Gathering for Women of Faith. She is a CLASS (Christian Leaders and Speakers Services) graduate and enjoys speaking to MOPS groups and women's events. Sherry lives with her husband, Ed, and their son, Logan, in southwest Virginia.

Rebecca Eims-Hinebaugh (Becky) was involved in MOPS leadership for twelve years. She has been married for thirty-two years and has two married daughters. Her daughters are now mothers attending MOPS groups, and Becky is enchanted with her three little granddaughters!

Jami English enjoys sharing her mothering experiences with the MOPS International family. She and her husband of seventeen years make their home with their two sons in Kenosha, Wisconsin.

Carla L. Foote is managing editor of leadership media at MOPS International. She lives with her husband and two children in Denver, Colorado.

Amy Gullion and her husband, Steve, live and work at a ranch for youth south of Alliance, Nebraska. Amy serves as an area coordinator for MOPS International and is the mother of three grown children.

Michele Hall has an educational and professional background in early childhood and curriculum development. Formerly vice president of ministry for MOPS International, Michele now lives with her family in Southern California.

Jeanette Hillman lives with her husband and two of their four children in the Middle East, where her husband pastors an international church. Across the United States, in Russia, and in the Middle East, Jeanette has spent twenty-five years leading women and helping them understand all they are in Christ. But her favorite job is being a mom.

Gretchen W. Jenkins serves as an area coordinator for MOPS International. After a season at home with three energetic boys, Gretchen is teaching computer to fourth through eighth graders.

Beth Jusino is a writer and the former general media managing editor of MOPS International. She lives in Denver, Colorado, with her husband, Eric.

Janis Kugler is director of major giving for MOPS International. Prior to coming to MOPS, she worked with Youth for Christ/USA and Officers' Christian Fellowship. She has a BS degree in business administration and an MBA. A Colorado native, Janis is married to her high school sweetheart, Steve, and has two daughters, Kelli and Karri. She lives in Littleton, Colorado.

Carol Kuykendall is the director of leadership development at MOPS International. She is the author of several books dealing with the early season of mothering and is a speaker, wife, and mother of three grown children.

Mary Beth Lagerborg (Beth) serves as media manager at MOPS International. She is coauthor of *Beyond Macaroni and Cheese* and *Once-*

a-Month Cooking. She and her husband live in Littleton, Colorado, and have three grown sons.

Dawn Lamuth-Higgins is the founder of Mommy Gear, an online boutique for breastfeeding families (www.mommygear.com). She is the mother of three bright, beautiful boys and enjoys writing, reading, and running.

Lori McCary helped establish the MOPS ministry in Russia and serves on the MOPS International Speakers' Bureau. She speaks to women's groups around the country and has a passion to see them discover God to be *everything* they need. Lori lives in The Woodlands, Texas, with her husband, Doug, and children, Russ, Sarah, Ryan, and Kate, who is newly adopted from China.

Lisa Moffitt is a business executive, respected community leader, wife, and mother of three children. Her humor and subtle advice help people recognize their value, the importance of their roles, and the breadth of their God-given influence. She participates in the MOPS International Speakers' Bureau.

Elisa Morgan, a mother of two and a new grandmother, is president and CEO of MOPS International. She is a popular author and speaker, and her daily radio program, *MOMSense*, is broadcast on more than seven hundred outlets nationwide. Her most recent book is *Naked Fruit: Getting Honest about the Fruit of the Spirit*. Elisa and her husband, Evan, live with their family in Centennial, Colorado.

Samantha Mulford-Phillips is an elementary school teacher in upstate New York. She has two children, Conner and Olivia, and serves as a MOPS ministry advancement coordinator for Zone 15 and England. "Daisy Chains" is based on her childhood in England.

Sandy Murphy's heart for families has led her to volunteer as an area coordinator for MOPS International and to work for years with missionary children in Kenya. Currently Sandy is an elementary teacher in Liverpool, New York, where she lives with her husband and two children.

Patti Nelson earned a bachelor's degree in human development and the family and special education, then gained hands-on experience mothering five children. She was instrumental in starting a MOPS group at her church and served as assistant event manager at MOPS International.

Rochelle Nelson and her husband, Pete, are raising their three sons with God's help and direction and own and operate a construction company in Buffalo, Minnesota. Rochelle has been involved with MOPS since 1992 and has a heart to help moms and to encourage leaders. She participates in the MOPS International Speakers' Bureau.

Charlotte Packard is a MOPS area coordinator living in Colorado Springs, Colorado. She and her husband, Mark, have three children, Grant, Denae, and Justin.

Karen Parks has served with MOPS International for over twenty years, first as a volunteer and then on staff for fifteen years, currently as director, strategic relations. Karen lives with her husband and three grown children in the foothills outside Denver.

Vicki M. Perry lives in Morgantown, West Virginia, with her husband, Richard, and children, Sarah, Elizabeth, and Benjamin. She enjoys being with family and friends and bike riding.

Andrea Peterson is wife to Steve and mother to Megan and Alexis. She has served in leadership in MOPS for more than eleven years. Andrea works in meeting and event planning and has a degree in business management.

Shelly A. Radic lives in Southern California, where she works from home as western regional coordinator for MOPS International. Raising four unique children provides plenty of writing inspiration. Shelly is the author of *The Birthday Book: Creative Ways to Celebrate Your Child's Special Day.*

Robyn Randall is a mom to three great kids—Zach, Justin, and Mackenzie—who love the Lord. She and her husband, Ted, are in ministry together in Redding, California.

Sylvia F. Reese has been involved with MOPS for thirteen years and is currently area coordinator for western Pennsylvania and West Virginia. She lives in Pittsburgh with her husband and two sons.

Rachel Ryan serves as media coordinator for MOPS International and has a passion for mothers of preschoolers. Rachel lives in Denver, Colorado.

Heather Rzepiennik is the mother of three and helped shape the Teen MOPS program for MOPS International.

Susie Sims is married to Kendall and mom to Stacey, Abbey, and Rebecca. She served as a group services representative for MOPS International and particularly enjoyed helping charter groups outside the United States. These pieces represent her first published writing.

Chris Ulshoffer credits her MOPS group for helping her through the early years of mothering twins. She has been married for twenty-five years and is the mother of four. She has served on the staff of MOPS International for eleven years.

Reneé Wheeler says, "God in his goodness has blessed me superabundantly above all I could ask with two wonderful children and two very special grandchildren. What a privilege it is to invest my life in theirs."

the MOPS story

● ● ● ● ● ● ● ● ● ● ● ● ● ● ●

YOU TAKE CARE OF YOUR CHILDREN, mom. Who takes care of you?

MOPS International (Mothers of Preschoolers) provides mothers of preschoolers with the nurture and resources they need to be the best moms they can be.

MOPS is dedicated to the message that "mothering matters," and that moms of young children need encouragement during these critical and formative years. Chartered groups meet in approximately 3,500 churches and Christian ministries throughout the United States and in twenty-nine other countries. Each MOPS program helps mothers find friendship and acceptance, provides opportunities for women to develop and practice leadership skills in the group, and promotes spiritual growth. The MOPPETS program offers a loving, learning experience for children while their moms attend MOPS. Other MOPS resources include *MOMSense* magazine and radio program, the MOPS

International website, and books and resources available through the MOPShop.

With 14.3 million mothers of preschoolers in the United States alone, many moms can't attend a local MOPS group. These moms still need the support that MOPS International can offer! For a small registration fee, any mother of preschoolers can join the MOPS♥to♥Mom Connection and receive *MOMSense* magazine six times a year, a weekly Mom-E-Mail message of encouragement, and other valuable benefits.

Find out how MOPS International can help you become part of the MOPS♥to♥Mom Connection, and/or join or start a MOPS group. Visit our website at www.MOPS.org. Phone us at 1-800-929-1287 or 303-733-5353. Or email Info@MOPS.org. To learn how to start a MOPS group, call 1-888-910-6677.